13

The Catholic Funeral

The Catholic Funeral

The Church's Ministry of Hope

Rev. Chris Aridas

A Crossroad Book
The Crossroad Publishing Company
New York

The Crossroad Publishing Company
370 Lexington Avenue, New York, NY 10017

Scripture quotations contained herein are from the
New Revised Standard Version Bible, © 1989 by the
Division of Christian Education of the National Council
of the Churches of Christ in the United States of America,
and are used by permission. All rights reserved.

Printed in the United States of America

Library of Congress Cataloging-in-Publication Data

Aridas, Chris, 1947-
    The Catholic funeral : the church's ministry of hope / Chris Aridas.
      p.   cm.
    ISBN 0-8245-1750-4 (pbk.)
    1. Funeral service—Catholic Church. 2. Catholic Church. Order of Christian
funerals. 3. Bereavement—Religious aspects—Catholic Church.   I. Title.
BX2035.6.F853A75   1998   98-11271
264'. 020985—dc21   CIP

1 2 3 4 5 6 7 8 9 10 03 02 01 00 99 98

*This book is dedicated to my parish's
Ministry of Hope wake teams,
whose dedication and inspiring service
have been a source of grace
for the entire parish.*

ACKNOWLEDGMENTS

Although I enjoy writing, working on a book has never been an easy task. The challenge of balancing my time as pastor, my personal life, and the additional work needed to pull together a manuscript by a particular date rivals the most complicated juggling act.

Several wonderful people, however, helped me accomplish the task at hand: Dennis Laderwager, my parish's Pastoral Associate, who assumed much of the "crisis management" that often occurs in a large suburban parish, thus granting me blocks of time to concentrate on writing; Fr. Don Hanson, Eppie Larke, Pat Molnar, and Bob Sturges, whose pastoral sensitivity for the bereaved provided much-needed insight when finalizing the manuscript; and Fr. John Worthley, whose work with terminally ill parishioners and families who were grieving was an inspiration and encouragement in putting the manuscript together. Finally, a special word of thanks to Robert Heller, longtime friend, for his support and encouragement throughout the process.

CONTENTS

INTRODUCTION

We're never ready. Regardless of how long a person lingers, regardless of the countless calls logged for ambulance assistance, regardless of the numerous conversations with hospice workers, doctors, relatives—we are never ready. The reality comes as a shock, an icy bucket of water dousing our passionate prayer for just one more day with the one we love.

Some, of course, pray for a speedy death for the one they love, one that doesn't involve suffering or lengthy periods of hospitalization or incapacitation. And yet, such a death leaves us who remain with so many loose threads, so many unspoken and unidentified feelings that one wonders which is worse and which is better, if, indeed, either can be seen as an acceptable alternative. We are simply never ready, whether we have been "prepared" over a long period of time or whether we receive an awful, unexpected phone call in the middle of the night. It always comes as a shock.

For this reason, you might find this book helpful in guiding you through some of the processes that surround our giving back to God someone we love. For example, if you wish to know more about the Church's teaching regarding life after death, you can turn to Chapter One, which will help you reflect on the Church's experience of

Christian hope and joy that embraces death as a natural part of our life in Christ.

In our contemporary Church, more and more people are actively planning and participating in the funeral liturgy of loved ones who have passed away. Chapter Two, therefore, gives a brief outline of the *Order of Christian Funerals*, explaining how each ritual fits a particular stage in the grieving process. Chapter Three then offers clear directions to those who wish to choose readings and/or participate as lectors in the Mass of Christian Burial. Each reading also has a brief reflection which you might use as a springboard for further personal reflection.

As the grieving process continues, individuals and families can use Chapter Four to understand their grief. Although not intended to be a "how-to" manual for the grieving process, the chapter does explore the insights of bereavement counselors who have helped others move through the grieving process toward a fuller experience of life here and now.

Chapter Five provides answers to many of the practicalities that confront families when planning a funeral. Here you will find suggestions, arranged in an easy Question and Answer format, for choosing a funeral home, arranging death notices, considering the donation of organs, acquiring cemetery plots, determining costs, etc. Although not all-encompassing regarding such topics, this section will provide you with a starting point in finding answers to some of these questions. It should save you time and anxiety during the hectic days preceding and following the funeral.

The Appendix includes a checklist for arranging a funeral as well as a diagram outlining the "small steps" we take when going through the five major stages of grieving. In addition, the Appendix also contains a brief narrative describing one parish's attempt to embrace the corporal works of mercy instructing us to bury the dead.

I offer this little book, therefore, as a source of ready information to help you in time of need. It will not answer all your questions, but, hopefully, will provide you with seeds of hope for reflection and growth during that inevitable time on life's journey when we are asked to give back to God the person we love.

CHAPTER ONE

DEATH COMES UNBIDDEN

> But we do not want you to be uninformed, brothers and
> sisters, about those who have died, so that you may not
> grieve as others do who have no hope. For since we
> believe that Jesus died and rose again, even so, through
> Jesus, God will bring with him those who have died.
> (1 Thessalonians 4:13-14)

IT SEEMS SO UNFAIR

We seek the wisdom and experience of the Church,
the community of believers, as we struggle with the
unspeakable difficulty of giving back to God the one we
love. For death itself seems so unfair, so final. If the
person we love had suffered a long time, death appears to
be the ultimate insult, depriving a person of his/her
dignity and humanity. We fight against the ignominy of
seeing a person we love deteriorate before our very eyes.
And then death comes—sometimes with a great struggle
that wrenches our heart, or in the darkness of uncon-
sciousness when a person no longer responds to our call,
or in the loneliness of an empty room when family and
friends have not yet arrived.

How can one embrace death with any peace when
the specter of death is so ghastly? How can one accept
the death of a loved one when we ourselves are overcome
by a sense of helplessness and emptiness because of
death's presence? And yet, the Christian community has
proclaimed repeatedly that death need not be victorious
over our feelings or our experience of life. As Pope John
Paul II instructs us in a talk at the 1997 World Youth Day
in Paris: "In the history of humanity Jesus Christ has
reversed the meaning of human existence. If everyday
experience shows us this experience as a passage toward
death, the paschal mystery opens to us the perspective of
a new life beyond death."

It is this paschal mystery—the dying and rising of
Christ—that remains key in our discussion of life after
death. As St. Paul reminds us in the First Letter to the
Corinthians:

> Now if Christ is proclaimed as raised from the dead, how
> can some of you say there is no resurrection of the dead?
> (1 Corinthians 15:12)

> But in fact Christ has been raised from the dead, the first
> fruits of those who have died. For since death came through
> a human being, the resurrection of the dead has also come
> through a human being. (1 Corinthians 15:20-21)

> But someone will ask, "How are the dead raised? With
> what kind of body do they come?" Fool! What you sow
> does not come to life unless it dies. And as for what you
> sow, you do not sow the body that is to be, but a bare
> seed, perhaps of wheat or of some other grain. But God
> gives it a body as he has chosen, and to each kind of seed
> its own body. (1 Corinthians 15:35-38)

> So it is with the resurrection of the dead. What is sown is
> perishable, what is raised is imperishable. It is sown in
> dishonor, it is raised in glory. It is sown in weakness, it is
> raised in power. It is sown a physical body, it is raised a
> spiritual body. If there is a physical body, there is also a
> spiritual body. (1 Corinthians 15:42-44)

Our Christian faith reminds us that death is not just
an unfortunate prelude to some pie-in-the-sky wish we
call resurrection. Rather, death, understood within the
paschal mystery, is the visible demonstration of the
deepest and most profound reality that transforms our
human situation because of that which has been achieved
through the Word made flesh.

JESUS: GOD WITH US

Christian tradition proclaims that our Lord has come
to show (reveal) God to us. Through this revelation, we
come to experience and embrace the very life of God;
that is, we come to know God as love poured out fully
and completely in an eternal act of self-giving. The
author of John's Gospel says it beautifully: "For God so
loved the world that he gave his only Son, so that
everyone who believes in him may not perish but may
have eternal life" (John 3:16). In order to show the full
depth of this love, in order to show the totality of this
self-gift, Jesus offered his life on the cross. Only through
such a gesture of selflessness could God reveal in Jesus
how total this love would be for all those who wished to
receive it.

This gesture of self-giving, however, was not meant
to be a manifestation of God's life apart from ours. It was

meant to be a revelation of what *our* life could be as we embrace God's life here and now, following the way of Jesus. This occurs "in the Spirit" whereby a Christian is able to embrace the same meaning Jesus assigned to the everyday experience of dying—culminating in the final experience of death.

> Do you not know that all of us who have been baptized into Christ Jesus were baptized into his death? Therefore we have been buried with him by baptism into death, so that, just as Christ was raised from the dead by the glory of the Father, so we too might walk in newness of life.
> For if we have been united with him in a death like his, we will certainly be united with him in a resurrection like his. But if we have died with Christ, we believe that we will also live with him. We know that Christ, being raised from the dead, will never die again; death no longer has dominion over him. (Romans 6:3-5, 8-9)

In another place, Paul reminds us that we are "always carrying in the body the death of Jesus, so that the life of Jesus may also be made visible in our bodies. For while we live, we are always being given up to death for Jesus' sake, so that the life of Jesus may be made visible in our mortal flesh" (2 Corinthians 4:10-11). This is the paschal mystery in action whereby we rely upon God's promise to do for us what God did in Christ, namely, to make our dying lives a joyful self-offering that reveals God's way of love.

This way of love takes place within the context of community, that is, as we relate to others in love by renouncing any desire to manage or possess another. This, therefore, is the task of all believers: to empty ourselves continually, as Jesus did, until we finally arrive at the point where we relinquish everything and anything not given fully to another.

Needless to say, we need not travel far and wide to relate to others in love, to embrace the paschal mystery. It happens repeatedly right where we are: within our families, workplace, neighborhood, community, etc. It occurs when a parent remains awake throughout the night comforting a frightened child; or an individual risks his/her job security by defending a wronged coworker; or an adult child cares for his/her dying father who had abused him/her in early childhood; or a teenager experiences the pain of rejection because he/she did not take drugs at a party. These are all everyday experiences of the paschal mystery—of the embrace of self-giving love to another. Such moments occur again and again for the purpose of creating one continuous thread of love throughout our life.

Such a self-offering reaches its culmination, however, at the point of death. It is here, having tried to surrender our very self to others, that we are given the opportunity to offer our body as the last piece of self-possession that we give to another. In doing so we finally can be other-centered—the Other being God whom we encounter at the point of death as the all-embracing experience of eternal love.

For the believer, therefore, death is not seen as a closed door that leads to an empty dark room. Rather, death is seen as that grace-filled awareness in which we, empty of every part of ourselves including our body, encounter God in total freedom, and present to God our final possession, our final gift of self, which God had given to us at the beginning of our life. This is the moment of gracious realization that only God, who fully and eternally empties God's self through Christ in the Spirit, can receive our gift of self regardless of how impoverished it might be. As we accept this realization and offer ourselves to God we experience eternal bliss, seeing God for who God is, eternal love. Perhaps this is what the poet T. S. Eliot meant in "East Coker," when he said, "In the end is my beginning."

REJECTING THE OFFER

For those who do not choose to give themselves to God, but have chosen to give themselves to the Evil One through a life of self-centeredness, the experience of hell unfolds in all its terror and despair. For, by our nature, we are called to give of our self, thus following the way of God. When we choose, however, to hold on to self by refusing to embrace the way of self-offering, we find ourselves in an eternal cycle of rejection. In giving ourselves to sin, therefore, we give ourselves to that which cannot receive our self-gift because a life of sin is already filled with self, thereby leaving no room, so to speak, to receive from another.

This is why the paschal mystery is so important in a Christian's life. It is only by embracing the dying/rising process revealed clearly in Jesus' own death and resurrection that we learn through our everyday experiences how to embrace God's eternal lifestyle now—a life of self-giving so that one's emptiness can be filled. The success of this lifestyle is proclaimed by St. Paul:

If then there is any encouragement in Christ, any
consolation from love, any sharing in the Spirit, any
compassion and sympathy, make my joy complete: be of
the same mind, having the same love, being in full
accord and of one mind. Do nothing from selfish
ambition or conceit, but in humility regard others as
better than yourselves. Let each of you look not to your
own interests, but to the interests of others. Let the same
mind be in you that was in Christ Jesus,

> who, though he was in the form of God,
>> did not regard equality with God
>> as something to be exploited,
> but emptied himself,
>> taking the form of a slave,
>> being born in human likeness.
> And being found in human form,
>> he humbled himself
>> and became obedient to the point
>>> of death—
>> even death on a cross.
> Therefore God also highly exalted him
>> and gave him the name
>> that is above every name,
> so that at the name of Jesus
>> every knee should bend,
>> in heaven and on earth and under
>>> the earth,
> and every tongue should confess
>> that Jesus Christ is Lord,
>> to the glory of God the Father.

(Philippians 2:1-11)

DEATH: THE NECESSARY PART OF LIFE'S JOURNEY

In God's plan, therefore, we must go through death
in order to come into wholeness, in order to come into

the final embrace we call love. During our earthly life we move in and out of that embrace, despite the ongoing opportunities given to enter fully into God's way of life. In death, however, we are finally removed from all distractions, all false realities and goals, so that we can choose God's way of life once and for all by presenting ourselves to God as a self-emptied and emptying being— clinging to nothing: no masks, no stereotypes, no pre-determined roles such as parent, spouse, child, laborer, etc. In death we are finally forced to be still, no longer struggling to move forward into the empty openness of time. In death a new life dawns for us that is the unceasing, intensively lived present; we move into God who is abiding love, forever offering, forever receiving, forever completing.

It is at the point of death, therefore, when we finally understand that God is not one of many persons outside of our consciousness, fighting for our attention. Rather, God is experienced as the very root of all that is—the ebb and flow of love outside of whom there is no-thing, no one. God is experienced, in the words of St. Paul, as our "all in all" (1 Corinthians 15:28): our past, present, and future. We discover in the overwhelming experience of death, in which we are invited to offer our final self-gift to another, that in the process of offering our gift, we regain our very identity from the One to whom we give ourselves. In short, we find ourselves in eternity when we give ourselves to that which is eternal, when we give ourselves to God who is love.

RESURRECTION HOPE

St. Paul reminds us that without resurrection, our faith is useless. Indeed, without resurrection our very life is useless, for we would not have any idea how we are called to live as human beings. Hoping in the resurrection, however, readies us for life in the here and now by revealing to us the result of living a life of love without reservation, that is, by revealing to us the result of Jesus' own life of self-offering.

Our hope of resurrection teaches us that we begin to embrace death not at the actual moment of physical death, but in the sundry ways our life is called to be a life of self-offering and self-gift for others. Except for the hope we have in resurrection, we would not have the courage to embrace this lifestyle. It is in this hope that we have the power of living God's life now, thus preparing us to accept fully God's life of self-offering at the point of death. This, again, involves our willingness to embrace the paschal mystery. As Mark states in his Gospel: "For those who want to save their life will lose it, and those who lose their life for my sake, and for the sake of the gospel, will save it" (Mark 8:35).

Resurrection hope also helps us who remain behind, for through our belief in the resurrection we realize that God's work of love does not cease when a person dies, but continues throughout eternity. This can bring us great comfort when struggling with unresolved issues that often emerge when a loved one dies—for example, words that were left unsaid, forgiveness which was not expressed, love which was not shown, hurts which were not

forgiven, etc. In a letter written to her friend Maurice
Bellière, St. Thérèse of Lisieux addresses this question
when she reminds her friend that those who have chosen
to offer themselves to God in death "participate also in
the infinite mercy of God," for in heaven those who have
died "remember that when they were fragile and mortal
like us they committed the same faults as we and went
through the same struggles, and their fraternal tenderness
becomes greater than it was on earth. That is why they
never stop protecting us and praying for us."

Resurrection hope, therefore, comforts us who
remain with the knowledge that God's gift of self-
emptying love continues within those who have died,
thereby guaranteeing that we who have undoubtedly
fallen short in our own relationship with our loved ones,
can be, and, indeed, are forgiven. Even more than
forgiven, we are now able to be loved as we had not been
loved by them before. We are now able to be loved as
God loves. St. Paul's words now take on new depth and
meaning: "Where, O death, is your victory? Where, O
death, is your sting?" (1 Corinthians 15:55).

CHAPTER TWO

THE ORDER OF CHRISTIAN FUNERALS

It is not the deceased who needs a funeral. We who are alive need a funeral. It brings together family and friends for mutual support and comfort, enabling them to share memories, tears, and celebratory rites of passage that give shape and expression to the experience of mourning.

The Church responds to this need in the *Order of Christian Funerals*, the beautiful expression of the Church's faith in the resurrection hope we have in Christ Jesus the Lord. With these prayers, the Church offers the grieving family the consolation and healing that comes through the grace of the Spirit and the faith of the community of believers. In doing so, we remind one another through words, gestures, and Christian symbols not to believe what we see—for we see death—but to see what we believe, that Jesus has conquered death, thus giving us hope that we will rise again.

The *Order* itself uses different rituals for different stages of the grieving process. Each ritual, also called a rite, comprises prayers, gestures, and symbols that help express and celebrate our faith in Jesus' victory over death and his presence with those who mourn.

THE VIGIL AND RELATED RITES AND PRAYERS

Rites Used before the Wake Service

There are three brief rites available to help the minister and others pray with the family and friends in the period right after death. The first two rites, "Prayers after Death" and "Gathering in the Presence of the Body," allow the community to express its concern for those who are grieving. Ideally, representatives of the community gather with the family to pray these prayers at the person's home or wherever the family congregates after the person is declared dead. This is an important opportunity for ministry because the time immediately following death is often one of confusion, disorientation, shock, and grief. With these prayers, the Church gently accompanies the mourners as they struggle with the initial adjustment to the fact of death, and to the grief that accompanies death.

A third rite, "Transfer of the Body to the Church or to the Place of Committal," is used just before the body is taken to the church for the funeral mass or to the place of committal. This latter time of prayer is brief—a prelude, so to speak, to the prayers offered at the church on the day of burial. Providing this prayer opportunity, however, often helps create a peaceful atmosphere for the family as they move to the church for the funeral liturgy.

Many parishes have arranged for teams of parishioners to pray one or more of these rites with the family, thus extending the arms of the Body of Christ to those who are mourning. This ministry brings great comfort to the family through the prayerful presence of the Christian community.

The Wake Service

The "Vigil for the Deceased," sometimes called the wake service, can take place in a person's home, a funeral home, or even in the church itself, provided that there is a suitable span of time between the vigil and the actual funeral mass. This is an opportunity for family and friends to show their concern by being present during the time of prayer. For those who are unable to attend the funeral mass because of work or other commitments, the Vigil for the Deceased offers the opportunity to pray with the family and to experience the healing power of God's promise as the readings and the prayers are shared.

Whenever possible, the family of the deceased can take part in the selection of the Scripture texts, and may serve as lectors or ministers during the wake service itself, unless grief prevents them from doing so in a comfortable fashion. During the wake service, families may offer a eulogy or remembrance of the deceased. Many find this experience very healing as they recount the ways the deceased has been a source of grace for family and friends.

THE FUNERAL LITURGY

The primary ritual used in burying the dead is the funeral liturgy which includes the "Funeral Mass" or the "Funeral Liturgy outside Mass." The latter ritual is used when a funeral mass is not permitted—for example, on holy days, during the Easter Triduum, or when a priest is unavailable to celebrate the funeral mass. This ritual is usually celebrated in the church, although it may take place in the home of the deceased, a funeral home, or a cemetery chapel.

In both rites, the Church uses the traditional Christian symbols that direct our attention to the Lord's power over death: holy water to remind us of our baptism; the white funeral pall, which signifies our Christian dignity; incense as a sign of honor to the body of the deceased, which became a temple of the Spirit at baptism; and the Easter candle to remind us of the Lord's victory over death and the Lord's continued presence in our midst. Depending upon local custom, a Book of the Gospels or a Bible may be placed on the coffin as a sign that Christians live by God's word, and that our fidelity to that word leads to eternal life. A cross is sometimes placed on the coffin to remind us of Jesus' suffering on the cross, which comes to victory in the resurrection.

Family members and friends can participate in either of these rituals by placing the symbols on the coffin, choosing and/or reading the Scripture texts, and offering the prayers of intercession. When a funeral mass is celebrated, family or friends may also bring the gifts to the altar and serve as ministers of the Eucharist, if they have been commissioned to do so.

THE RITE OF COMMITTAL

The "Rite of Commital" is the faith community's final act in caring for the body of the deceased. It is usually celebrated at the grave, tomb, or crematorium. In this rite, the community expresses its hope that those marked with the sign of faith in baptism will indeed experience the glory of the resurrection. As the deceased passes from the sight of those who remain here on earth, we commend them to the communion of saints in heaven. In many parishes, representatives of the parish community participate in this ritual, leading the final prayers for the mourners.

HOW TO PARTICIPATE IN THE *ORDER OF CHRISTIAN FUNERALS*

Family members are invited to participate in the different rituals of the *Order of Christian Funerals* in a variety of ways. The degree of participation, however, is left up to the family. For the most part, however, family members have found that actively participating in the various rituals—for example, offering a eulogy at the wake service, choosing and/or reading Scripture texts at the funeral mass, or bringing the gifts to the altar during the funeral mass—has been a source of grace and consolation for them. Many parishes have trained teams of parishioners to help families make these choices. Although many do find this helpful, others find it is more than they can manage. If that be the case, allow the priest or the parish's bereavement team to make those choices for you. They are there to serve you so that you may mourn in the way that is best for you.

CHAPTER THREE

SCRIPTURE READINGS

It is through God's word that we find peace and consolation, hence, the Church's desire to have the Word of God read at all funeral liturgies. When choosing a passage to read, try to give yourself time to review all of them. It may appear that you have no heart or desire to spend time reading. After all, there are so many details and people to whom you must give your attention. The quiet time you give yourself in reviewing the Scripture readings, however, will be a way of receiving a special gift from God. The Lord will speak to your heart as you give the Spirit time to allow the Scripture passages to unfold their comforting grace within your being. After each passage, there is a brief reflection that, hopefully, will assist you in your time of prayer.

When choosing passages to be proclaimed at the funeral liturgy, you have several options. You may choose one Old Testament and/or one New Testament reading. Either or both may be read by a family member or friend, if you so desire. In addition, you can choose one Gospel reading, which is always read by a priest or deacon. Since the Responsorial Psalm is usually sung after the First Reading, only the refrains have been listed.

The same is true of the Gospel Alleluia, which is sung before the Gospel proclamation. If you have a particular refrain or verse you would like to use, your parish's music minister should be able to accommodate your choice.

You will note that most of the Scripture passages have numbers in parentheses following each citation. The numbers that have a hyphen indicate where the reading may be found in the lectionary; the underlined numbers indicate where the passage can be found in the *Order of Christian Funerals*, thus facilitating your ability to communicate your choices to the celebrant. In that I prefer the New Revised Standard Version Bible—a translation of Scripture approved by the American Catholic bishops—I have chosen that translation for all the passages in this section.

OLD TESTAMENT READINGS

JOB 19:1, 23-27 (789-1/83)

> Then Job answered:
> O that my words were written down!
> O that they were inscribed in a book!
> O that with an iron pen and with lead
> they were engraved on a rock forever!
> For I know that my Redeemer lives,
> and that at the last he will stand upon the earth;
> and after my skin has been thus destroyed,
> then in my flesh I shall see God,
> whom I shall see on my side,
> and my eyes shall behold, and not another.
> My heart faints within me!

Our whole body feels faint. We don't know what our next step will be. It's so overwhelming. We know what God's word tells us: "My Redeemer lives!" Right now, however, they just appear as words on a page. The iron pen has already written its terrible message on our heart. We've lost the one we love. All we can see is the name chiseled on a tombstone standing stark and cold in what has become a daily nightmare. "For I know that my Redeemer lives," God's word keeps telling us. But do we really know? Right now we are not sure of anything except the pain, the loss, the confusion. If only the Lord would show us that he lives. We so want to believe and know the truth of that word, the fullness of that promise. What prayer might we make in such turmoil?

"Lord, let me seek you through this pain and allow your love to embrace me. I have nothing to offer but the confusion and the anger and the loss. It's all I have right now. I wish I could give you nice feelings of trust and belief, but I can't. If I don't give you the pain and the confusion and the loss, I won't be able to give you my heart, for right now my heart is filled only with those feelings that I don't want to call my own. But they are mine, and so I offer them to you, so you might make them yours."

WISDOM 3:1-9 (789-2/84)

But the souls of the righteous are in the hand of God,
and no torment will ever touch them.
In the eyes of the foolish they seemed to have died,
and their departure was thought to be a disaster,
and their going from us to be their destruction;
but they are at peace.
For though in the sight of others they were punished,
their hope is full of immortality.
Having been disciplined a little, they will receive
     great good,
because God tested them and found them worthy
     of himself;
like gold in the furnace he tried them,
and like a sacrificial burnt offering he accepted them.
In the time of their visitation they will shine forth,
and will run like sparks through the stubble.
They will govern nations and rule over peoples,
and the Lord will reign over them forever.
Those who trust in him will understand truth,
and the faithful will abide with him in love,
because grace and mercy are upon his holy ones,
and he watches over his elect.

We know from experience the joy of holding the hand of someone we love. There's a sense of security and comfort as we grasp and are grasped by the one we love. Whether it be our spouse, our child, our parent, our friend, our brother, or our sister, holding someone's hand brings back memories of joy-filled vacations, of quiet walks down lovers' lane, of new adventures made safe by the hand who held us tightly, of healing moments when we held the person's hand through sickness, and of final farewells as we squeezed ever so gently the hand of one whose own hand was reaching toward God. The Scriptures, therefore, offer us comfort, assuring us that our beloved are "in the hand of God, and no torment will ever touch them." Though difficult to offer back to God the one we love, we know that this "offering" is really a transferring of one hand to another, from one beloved to another Beloved. Know also that God wishes to hold our hand during this time, so that God might remain in the center, standing between us and our loved one—holding both of us by our hands as we each continue our journeys with the Lord at our side.

WISDOM 4:7-14 (789-3/<u>85</u>)

But the righteous, though they die early, will be at rest.
For old age is not honored for length of time,
or measured by number of years;
but understanding is gray hair for anyone,
and a blameless life is ripe old age.
There were some who pleased God and were loved
by him,
and while living among sinners were taken up.

They were caught up so that evil might not change
  their understanding
or guile deceive their souls.
For the fascination of wickedness obscures what
  is good,
and roving desire perverts the innocent mind.
Being perfected in a short time, they fulfilled
  long years;
for their souls were pleasing to the Lord,
therefore he took them quickly from the midst of
  wickedness.

Throughout history, God's people struggled to understand God's plan when a young person died. In an ancient culture that equated long life with God's favor, the people of Israel had to make sense of the senseless death of a young person. Although we do not live in the same cultural milieu as our ancestors in faith, we too struggle in a similar way. Intellectually we are more comfortable with the death of an older person whose life fulfilled long years, than the death of a young person whose life was cut short through sickness or accident. Such a tragedy leaves us with the same unanswered question raised by the people in the Old Testament: Why does God do such a thing? The Book of Wisdom tries to offer an answer, although it may appear less than satisfactory. We're reminded that those who die early will be at rest; that God called them because they were loved by the Lord; that "their souls were pleasing to the Lord" who "took them quickly from the midst of wickedness." You can see from the brief passage that sometimes there really are no answers that satisfy our yearning for clarity. We can only be certain that God's plan for us always

involves life—true life, which transcends whatever we
might think life is all about in this world. The Scripture
author had no neat, feel-good answer: only faith in God's
plan and God's love. Sometimes that's all we have, and
that's the most difficult thing to accept.

ISAIAH 25:6A, 7-9 (789-4/86)

> On this mountain the Lord of hosts will make for
>   all peoples
>   a feast of rich food, a feast of well-aged wines.
> And he will destroy on this mountain
>   the shroud that is cast over all peoples,
>   the sheet that is spread over all nations;
>   he will swallow up death forever.
> Then the Lord God will wipe away the tears from
>   all faces,
>   and the disgrace of his people he will take away
>   from all the earth,
>   for the Lord has spoken.
> It will be said on that day,
>   Lo, this is our God; we have waited for him, so
>   that he might save us.
>   This is the Lord for whom we have waited;
>   let us be glad and rejoice in his salvation.

God's people hoped for the day when the messiah
would provide for their every need. Using poetic terms,
the prophet Isaiah describes this time as a banquet, a time
of feasting, a time when tears will be dried and death will
be conquered. The "mountain" in the passage probably
refers to the holy city, Jerusalem, which, built on a
mountain, was considered the sacred place of God's
dwelling.

For the Christian, however, the prophet's words take on a deeper meaning. The banquet is the Eucharist, meant to nurture and strengthen us on life's journey. The mountain on which all this happens is Calvary, where our Lord conquered sin and death by his own death on the cross. What we fear most, the "shroud that is cast over all," is torn asunder on that mountain where our God offered his life so we might live; where our God offered his death so that we might never die. God's word, therefore, offers us comfort, reminding us that in the death of the believer is the manifestation of "the Lord for whom we have waited."

LAMENTATIONS 3:17-26 (789-5/87)

My soul is bereft of peace;
    I have forgotten what happiness is;
so I say, "Gone is my glory, and all that I had hoped
        for from the Lord."
The thought of my affliction and my homelessness
    is wormwood and gall!
My soul continually thinks of it
    and is bowed down within me.
But this I call to mind,
    and therefore I have hope:
The steadfast love of the Lord never ceases,
    his mercies never come to an end;
they are new every morning;
    great is your faithfulness.
"The Lord is my portion," says my soul,
    "therefore I will hope in him."
The Lord is good to those who wait for him,
    to the soul that seeks him.

> It is good that one should wait quietly
>   for the salvation of the Lord.

Right now we feel the words "bereft of peace" in the depth of our being. We probably have never seen or tasted "wormwood and gall," but the words sure sound like what we're experiencing through the tears. Even the title of this Old Testament book summarizes our feelings: *Lamentations.* The Scripture author knows exactly what we're feeling, indicated by the honest and poignant cry from the heart: "I have forgotten what happiness is."

Yet through it all there is hope. Unexpected, unexplained, but there nonetheless. "The steadfast love of the Lord never ceases." How might that be? How can an author whose words so vividly capture the feeling of desolation and abandonment experienced through death maintain that God's steadfast love never ceases? Is the author trying to reveal something that we cannot see through the tears and the pain? " 'The Lord is my portion,' says my soul, 'therefore I will hope in him.' " If only we could have that trust and faith and hope. If only we could "wait quietly." But the details surrounding funeral preparations, the exhausting experience of shared tears, the noise of people's words we don't remember have pushed away any chance to "wait quietly." The time will come, however. Right now it may seem impossible, but the time will come.

DANIEL 12:1-3 (789-6/88)

> At that time Michael, the great prince, the protector of
> your people, shall arise. There shall be a time of anguish,

such as has never occurred since nations first came into
existence. But at that time your people shall be delivered,
everyone who is found written in the book. Many of
those who sleep in the dust of the earth shall awake,
some to everlasting life, and some to shame and
everlasting contempt. Those who are wise shall shine
like the brightness of the sky, and those who lead many
to righteousness, like the stars forever and ever.

Traditionally, we associate Michael the Archangel
with protection and comfort. As children we prayed for
him to "defend us in battle. . . ." Today, more than ever
before, we need a defender as we battle for our life, now
changed in a way we never thought possible. The future
looks dark, but God's word gives us a promise: those
who die "shall shine like the brightness of the sky."

Imagine! Every time we gaze at the heavens and see
the stars shining brightly, piercing the dark vastness of
the unknown beyond the sky, we can recall God's
promise. Just as Noah saw in the rainbow arching the
heavens the memory of God's faithfulness, we too can
see in the stars above a personal sign from God given to
believers, lest the darkness of grief consume us.

2 MACCABEES 12:43-45 (789-7/89)

He also took up a collection, man by man, to the amount
of two thousand drachmas of silver, and sent it to
Jerusalem to provide for a sin offering. In doing this he
acted very well and honorably, taking account of the
resurrection. For if he were not expecting that those who
had fallen would rise again, it would have been superflu-
ous and foolish to pray for the dead. But if he was

> looking to the splendid reward that is laid up for those
> who fall asleep in godliness, it was a holy and pious
> thought. Therefore he made atonement for the dead, so
> that they might be delivered from their sin.

In this passage, our Catholic community finds the root of our tradition that encourages us to pray for the dead. Some, unfortunately, veer away from such prayer, thinking it both senseless and useless. After all, they would argue, what's done is done. How can prayer today help those who have died? Nonetheless, Scripture tells us that those who offer such prayer act "honorably, taking account of the resurrection." This, of course, is the key. Resurrection.

More than simply a passage about praying for the dead, the Scripture intends to emphasize our belief in resurrection. Faith tells us that our life with Christ does not end when we die. It begins in a new and vibrant way because of our hope in resurrection. Prayer for the dead, therefore, continues to touch those who have died because it unites our prayer with the eternal prayer of Jesus, who constantly intercedes before the throne of God. In doing so, something important happens to us as well. We receive the grace of intercession, giving us greater assurance of God's compassion and love as we unite our will with God's desire to have all brought to the fullness of life in Jesus.

NEW TESTAMENT READINGS

ACTS 10:34-43 (790-1/90)

> Then Peter began to speak to them: "I truly understand
> that God shows no partiality, but in every nation anyone
> who fears him and does what is right is acceptable to
> him. You know the message he sent to the people of
> Israel, preaching peace by Jesus Christ—he is Lord of
> all. That message spread throughout Judea, beginning in
> Galilee after the baptism that John announced: how God
> anointed Jesus of Nazareth with the Holy Spirit and with
> power; how he went about doing good and healing all
> who were oppressed by the devil, for God was with him.
> We are witnesses to all that he did both in Judea and in
> Jerusalem. They put him to death by hanging him on a
> tree; but God raised him on the third day and allowed
> him to appear, not to all the people but to us who were
> chosen by God as witnesses, and who ate and drank with
> him after he rose from the dead. He commanded us to
> preach to the people and to testify that he is the one
> ordained by God as judge of the living and the dead. All
> the prophets testify about him that everyone who
> believes in him receives forgiveness of sins through his
> name."

How incredibly comforting to know that "everyone
who believes in him [Jesus] receives forgiveness of sins
through his name." This passage recounts the story of
Jesus in a condensed form, indicating how God the
Father worked through Jesus his Son so that "in every
nation anyone who fears him [Jesus] and does what is
right is acceptable to him." As we prepare ourselves for
the difficult task of giving back to God the person we
love, we cling to this promise, that even in our weakness

and sinfulness, we are acceptable to God when we strive to do what is right. Although no one comes before the Father having achieved a state of perfection based on his/ her own merits, all of us can come before the Father perfected in our relationship with God because Jesus "is Lord of all." This is the grace that is given freely because God's love for us is everlasting.

ROMANS 5:5-11 (790-2/91)

> And hope does not disappoint us, because God's love has been poured into our hearts through the Holy Spirit that has been given to us.
> For while we were still weak, at the right time Christ died for the ungodly. Indeed, rarely will anyone die for a righteous person—though perhaps for a good person someone might actually dare to die. But God proves his love for us in that while we still were sinners Christ died for us. Much more surely then, now that we have been justified by his blood, will we be saved through him from the wrath of God. For if while we were enemies, we were reconciled to God through the death of his Son, much more surely, having been reconciled, will we be saved by his life. But more than that, we even boast in God through our Lord Jesus Christ, through whom we have now received reconciliation.

What does God's love accomplish for us? According to St. Paul, two separate, though connected, gifts are given us. The first is the gift of justification, often called righteousness. We are put in a right relationship with God, which means we once again experience the gift of sonship or daughtership, freely given us in Jesus. The second gift given us is the gift of reconciliation. This means that we who are God's sons and daughters are joined to the Lord in an intimate relationship which makes us one with the God. All this takes place because Jesus died for us. St. Paul then reminds us that if such a great gift were given through Jesus' death, how much more will we be given through Jesus' life? The answer, of course, is that we will be given more than we can imagine: we will be given eternal life, resurrection life, life with God forever.

ROMANS 5:17-21 (790-3/92)

If, because of the one man's trespass, death exercised dominion through that one, much more surely will those who receive the abundance of grace and the free gift of righteousness exercise dominion in life through the one man, Jesus Christ.

Therefore just as one man's trespass led to condemnation for all, so one man's act of righteousness leads to justification and life for all. For just as by the one man's disobedience the many were made sinners, so by the one man's obedience the many will be made righteous. But law came in, with the result that the trespass multiplied; but where sin increased, grace abounded all the more, so that, just as sin exercised dominion in death, so grace might also exercise dominion through justification leading to eternal life through Jesus Christ our Lord.

St. Paul's Letter to the Romans contains some of our Catholic tradition's most difficult Scripture passages. Although very dense in terms of intellectual content, they do offer us an exciting doorway to the wonders of God's plan for those who have accepted Jesus. Underneath the difficult concepts that use unfamiliar words and phrases, lies the core of our hope, namely, that Christ the Lord has conquered death once and for all. What a relief to know that the greatest fear of our life—the fear that our very existence ends at the point of death—has been put to rest through Jesus' own death and resurrection.

ROMANS 6:3-9 (790-4/93)

> Do you not know that all of us who have been baptized into Christ Jesus were baptized into his death? Therefore we have been buried with him by baptism into death, so that, just as Christ was raised from the dead by the glory of the Father, so we too might walk in newness of life.
>
> For if we have been united with him in a death like his, we will certainly be united with him in a resurrection like his. We know that our old self was crucified with him so that the body of sin might be destroyed, and we might no longer be enslaved to sin. For whoever has died is freed from sin. But if we have died with Christ, we believe that we will also live with him. We know that Christ, being raised from the dead, will never die again; death no longer has dominion over him.

Most of us do not remember our baptism. We don't remember the beautiful prayers and powerful symbols that surrounded that life-giving moment on our journey of faith: the sacred oil on our body, the shock of cold water hitting our foreheads like a hammer (or the loss of control we felt if we were immersed in the baptismal pool), the candle's brightness representing Christ's resurrection, the feeling of starched newness on the lacy baptismal garment, and the poetic images of darkness and light that framed the baptismal prayers. Nevertheless, our baptism provided us with life's primary reference point on our journey of faith: for in baptism we were united with Jesus' death so we might be united to Jesus' resurrection.

The thread present in both baptism and this passage from Romans, therefore, is the image of dying and rising. We experience that reality again and again in the everyday, ordinary deaths that are part of our life. As Christians, we believe that these everyday deaths are a precursor to the final death, which brings us life. As we learn to embrace the everyday deaths with the love of Christ—the deaths that enabled us to die to self through acts of forgiveness, charity, and selfless giving—we learn to embrace such deaths for what they are: reminders that we who have died in Christ day after day will live with him forever.

ROMANS 8:14-23 (790-5/94)

For all who are led by the Spirit of God are children of God. For you did not receive a spirit of slavery to fall back into fear, but you have received a spirit of adoption. When we cry, "Abba! Father!" it is that very Spirit bearing witness with our spirit that we are children of God, and if children, then heirs, heirs of God and joint heirs with Christ—if, in fact, we suffer with him so that we may also be glorified with him.

I consider that the sufferings of this present time are not worth comparing with the glory about to be revealed to us. For the creation waits with eager longing for the

revealing of the children of God; for the creation was
subjected to futility, not of its own will but by the will of
the one who subjected it, in hope that the creation itself
will be set free from its bondage to decay and will obtain
the freedom of the glory of the children of God. We
know that the whole creation has been groaning in labor
pains until now; and not only the creation, but we
ourselves, who have the first fruits of the Spirit, groan
inwardly while we wait for adoption, the redemption of
our bodies.

Sometimes the suffering we see others endure as they
embrace the mystery of death can be excruciating. Our
heart breaks knowing that someone we love is experiencing pain that we cannot quell. Often it is more than we
can bear, especially when watching a parent or beloved
aunt or uncle or grandparent deteriorate before our very
eyes. We feel helpless knowing the helplessness they are
feeling. It appears so dehumanizing and unfair.

For that very reason, St. Paul's words offer us hope
and courage by giving us a vision and picture of that
which is yet to come. He begins by stating the fact of our
human existence: we suffer the pangs of futility and
bondage, which he likens to labor pains. Despite this
reality, Paul reminds us that because of God's Spirit, we
are "heirs of God and joint heirs with Christ." He then
makes an unbelievable assertion, stating that the suffering
experienced in this life is barely worth a thought when
we remember the glory that is yet to come. In other
words, we know through the dying and rising revealed in
Christ Jesus that the suffering experienced in this life is
part of God's plan for us to die and rise, following the

pattern of Jesus' own death and resurrection. Think of the implications layered in this passage: we are heirs to God's kingdom, heirs to God's life-giving plan, heirs to the Spirit of sonship and daughtership freely and graciously given us in Jesus.

Will this truth make the suffering disappear, or alleviate the pain that our body endures, or enable us to ignore the heartbreak of seeing someone we love endure his/her suffering? Of course not! Faith does not exempt us from the pain of dying, but raises our expectation "while we wait for adoption, the redemption of our bodies."

ROMANS 8:31B-35, 37-39 (790-6/95)

If God is for us, who is against us? He who did not withhold his own Son, but gave him up for all of us, will he not with him also give us everything else? Who will bring any charge against God's elect? It is God who justifies. Who is to condemn? It is Christ Jesus, who died, yes, who was raised, who is at the right hand of God, who indeed intercedes for us. Who will separate us from the love of Christ? Will hardship, or distress, or persecution, or famine, or nakedness, or peril, or sword?

No, in all these things we are more than conquerors through him who loved us. For I am convinced that neither death, nor life, nor angels, nor rulers, nor things present, nor things to come, nor powers, nor height, nor depth, nor anything else in all creation, will be able to separate us from the love of God in Christ Jesus our Lord.

Right now God doesn't seem to be in the picture at all. All we can think about is the painful experience of separation that fills every waking moment. Nevertheless, though we may not be caring much about God right now, it is important to remain rooted in God's love during this time. By doing so, a most amazing thing takes place. We discover in God's love the full experience of the one who died. In fact, as we turn to the Lord, relying on his love for us and our loved one, we will be able to come closer than ever before to the person who died. It may sound strange, but the fact remains: in Christ's love, we can experience all love, including the love of those who have gone before us. As St. Paul confidently proclaims: "He who did not withhold his own Son, but gave him up for all of us, will he not with him also give us everything else?" That is the promise God offers. He will give us everything that we need, proven by the life of Jesus, which already has been given. Would the God who gave himself to us deprive us of our beloved's presence and love? Impossible. He provides it anew in the love we experience through Christ Jesus the Lord.

ROMANS 14:7-9, 10B-12 (790-7/96)

We do not live to ourselves, and we do not die to ourselves. If we live, we live to the Lord, and if we die, we die to the Lord; so then, whether we live or whether we die, we are the Lord's. For to this end Christ died and lived again, so that he might be Lord of both the dead and the living.

For we will all stand before the judgment seat of God. For it is written,

> "As I live, says the Lord, every knee shall bow
>   to me,
>   and every tongue shall give praise to God."

So then, each of us will be accountable to God.

"Whether we live or whether we die, we are the Lord's." The comforting truth of God's word enfolds us: embraced passionately by our God, we cannot be separated from him! Branded by the seal of the Spirit in baptism, "we are the Lord's." This is not meant to suggest that God owns us as we might own a piece of property. Rather, it is meant to affirm the ownership of love. In order to understand this, we look at our own experience. Think of a time when someone we love did something wrong. The ownership of love enabled us to stand with the person regardless of the offense. This is even more true for God. "For to this end Christ died and lived again, so that he might be Lord of both the dead and the living." God's ownership of love extends beyond this life into the life that follows death, enabling him to stand by us because he is the Lord of both the dead and the living.

1 CORINTHIANS 15:20-24A, 25-28 (790-8/97)

But in fact Christ has been raised from the dead, the first fruits of those who have died. For since death came through a human being, the resurrection of the dead has also come through a human being; for as all die in Adam, so all will be made alive in Christ. But each in his own order: Christ the first fruits, then at his coming those who belong to Christ. Then comes the end, when he hands

over the kingdom to God the Father. For he must reign
until he has put all his enemies under his feet. The last
enemy to be destroyed is death. For "God has put all
things in subjection under his feet." But when it says,
"All things are put in subjection," it is plain that this does
not include the one who put all things in subjection under
him. When all things are subjected to him, then the Son
himself will also be subjected to the one who put all
things in subjection under him, so that God may be all in
all.

"For as all die in Adam, so all will be made alive in
Christ." No one needs to convince us that "all die."
Although we know that no one escapes its grasp, we
spend most of our life trying to convince ourselves that
we will elude death—or at the very least, forestall it in
some fashion. Confronted by the death of someone we
love, however, the reality of death breaks through our
defenses, taking advantage of our vulnerability and fears.
Why did it happen? What kind of God would let someone
suffer like this? How come God couldn't give us more
time? What kind of God would take a child? These are
only some of the questions which surface, only to be
submerged when no satisfactory answer appears.

At this time it would be helpful to remember the
remainder of the sentence Paul writes to the people in
Corinth: ". . . so all will be made alive in Christ." Here
we again encounter the word *all*, the same word used to
describe the reality of death that is part and parcel of our
humanity ("all die in Adam"). Paul, however, now
employs it as a way of introducing us to the unexpected
gift that is ours because "in fact Christ has been raised
from the dead." This gift is given us "so that God may be

all in all." When confronted with the mystery of death,
Paul reminds us to trust the mystery of life shared with us
in Jesus' own death and resurrection.

1 CORINTHIANS 15:51-57 (790-9/98)

> Listen, I will tell you a mystery! We will not all die, but
> we will all be changed, in a moment, in the twinkling of
> an eye, at the last trumpet. For the trumpet will sound,
> and the dead will be raised imperishable, and we will be
> changed. For this perishable body must put on imperish-
> ability, and this mortal body must put on immortality.
> When this perishable body puts on imperishability, and
> this mortal body puts on immortality, then the saying that
> is written will be fulfilled:
>
>> "Death has been swallowed up in victory."
>> "Where, O death, is your victory?
>>   Where, O death, is your sting?"
>
> The sting of death is sin, and the power of sin is the law.
> But thanks be to God, who gives us the victory through
> our Lord Jesus Christ.

The sublime music of Handel's *Messiah* enhances
the power of this familiar Scripture text. As part of our
reflection, it might be worthwhile listening again to
Handel's musical portrait of the text. Through the music,
we can feel the transforming power of the Scripture
verses as the music soars repetitively, like a spiral
staircase aiming our sights higher and higher to the full
meaning of resurrection life. Note that Paul is not
speaking about a life prolonged, but a life transformed.
Reflect on the contrasting images: imperishable/perish-

able and immortal/mortal. Ironically, death is the un-
avoidable doorway to a life that God's love transforms.
With Paul, therefore, we can say, "Thanks be to God,
who gives us the victory through our Lord Jesus Christ."

2 CORINTHIANS 4:14—5:1

> Because we know that the one who raised the Lord Jesus
> will raise us also with Jesus, and will bring us with you
> into his presence. Yes, everything is for your sake, so that
> grace, as it extends to more and more people, may
> increase thanksgiving, to the glory of God.
>
> So we do not lose heart. Even though our outer
> nature is wasting away, our inner nature is being renewed
> day by day. For this slight momentary affliction is
> preparing us for an eternal weight of glory beyond all
> measure, because we look not at what can be seen but at
> what cannot be seen; for what can be seen is temporary,
> but what cannot be seen is eternal.
>
> For we know that if the earthly tent we live in is
> destroyed, we have a building from God, a house not
> made with hands, eternal in the heavens.

It's very hard to believe that "everything is for your
sake." How could the pain, the disorientation, the anger,
and the fear we experience while burying someone we
love be for our sake? What kind of God would do this to
someone he loves? Doesn't God see what's happening?
Doesn't God see the tears, hear the sobs, know the pain
for those who are left behind?

St. Paul gives us an answer to our question: "For this
slight momentary affliction is preparing us for an eternal
weight of glory beyond all measure, because we look not

at what can be seen but at what cannot be seen; for what can be seen is temporary, but what cannot be seen is eternal." Allow me to offer my personal paraphrase of this sentence: Do not believe what you see, but see what you believe. If we look at what we see, we see death with its apparent finality. However, that is true only in the eyes of the world. In God's eyes, death no longer exists; it is quite temporary, having been destroyed by Jesus' own death and resurrection. Therefore, with St. Paul, pray for the grace to see with God's eyes: to see the eternity of life given us through God's gracious gift of Jesus.

2 CORINTHIANS 5:1, 6-10 (790-10/99)

> For we know that if the earthly tent we live in is destroyed, we have a building from God, a house not made with hands, eternal in the heavens.
>
> So we are always confident; even though we know that while we are at home in the body we are away from the Lord—for we walk by faith, not by sight. Yes, we do have confidence, and we would rather be away from the body and at home with the Lord. So whether we are at home or away, we make it our aim to please him. For all of us must appear before the judgment seat of Christ, so that each may receive recompense for what has been done in the body, whether good or evil.

We spend a lifetime preserving this "earthly tent we live in." Then it happens. An accident, sickness, or old age begins to undo everything we've sought to accomplish. We try to stop the process, but it pushes forward without our help and despite our efforts to the contrary.

As that takes place, we have a choice to make. Will we insist upon walking our own way even if it causes us to stumble, or will we begin to walk "by faith," confident that God has prepared for us "a house not made with hands, eternal in the heavens"? Walking by faith during this time is difficult. It goes against the grain. The goal to keep in mind, however, is that "we make it our aim to please him." How might we please our God during this time of separation and grief? you might ask. By continuing on our life's journey remembering not just the one whom we love, but the One who loves us.

PHILIPPIANS 3:20-21 (790-11/100)

> But our citizenship is in heaven, and it is from there that we are expecting a Savior, the Lord Jesus Christ. He will transform the body of our humiliation that it may be conformed to the body of his glory, by the power that also enables him to make all things subject to himself.

As always, we look to the Lord. In him we see both "the body of our humiliation" as well as "the body of his [Jesus'] glory." Paul offers this radical contrast as a word of encouragement. When speaking of this "body of our humiliation," however, Paul does not mean to denigrate the human body. Rather, he simply wishes to acknowledge the fact that our body dies, even though we try everything in our power to prevent that from happening. Knowing that his "citizenship is in heaven," Paul embraces the fact of death without fear, giving him hope to believe that he will be "conformed to the body of his [Jesus'] glory."

This, then, is our prayer: to trust that our heavenly citizenship papers have been ratified by the Lord. Through his death and resurrection, he makes us citizens of the kingdom, something we could not attain on our own. This is true for us who remain and for those who have gone before us. Being citizens of the same kingdom, we will surely encounter one another again.

1 THESSALONIANS 4:13-18 (790-12/<u>101</u>)

> But we do not want you to be uninformed, brothers and sisters, about those who have died, so that you may not grieve as others do who have no hope. For since we believe that Jesus died and rose again, even so, through Jesus, God will bring with him those who have died. For this we declare to you by the word of the Lord, that we who are alive, who are left until the coming of the Lord, will by no means precede those who have died. For the Lord himself, with a cry of command, with the archangel's call and with the sound of God's trumpet, will descend from heaven, and the dead in Christ will rise first. Then we who are alive, who are left, will be caught up in the clouds together with them to meet the Lord in the air; and so we will be with the Lord forever. Therefore encourage one another with these words.

I find it encouraging to remember that in the early Church, even though the people lived during the very time when Jesus walked with them in the flesh, there were still believers who "grieved as those who had no hope." We sometimes think that our own grief shows a lack of faith, when in reality, it's a natural, human response to the separation we experience through death.

It is unrealistic to think that faith makes the feelings of separation disappear. It was not true in the early Church and is not true today.

What is true, however, is the importance of Paul's reminder to "encourage one another," for no one need go through the process of grieving alone. Family and friends, bereavement groups, prayer groups, etc., are the channels of grace God gives for those who grieve. They are the source of encouragement of which Paul speaks. Regardless of how you are feeling, therefore, allow God's channels of grace to nourish and support you during this time. Seek them out lest you remain uninformed about those who have died.

2 TIMOTHY 2:8-13 (790-13/102)

> Remember Jesus Christ, raised from the dead, a descendant of David—that is my gospel, for which I suffer hardship, even to the point of being chained like a criminal. But the word of God is not chained. Therefore I endure everything for the sake of the elect, so that they may also obtain the salvation that is in Christ Jesus, with eternal glory. The saying is sure:
>
>> If we have died with him, we will also live
>>   with him;
>> if we endure, we will also reign with him;
>> if we deny him, he will also deny us;
>> if we are faithless, he remains faithful—
>> for he cannot deny himself.

"If we have died with him, we will also live with him." How can we die with Jesus? Does Paul mean physical suffering and death, as in the suffering which Jesus endured on the cross? It would be understandable for us to equate our human suffering with a dying with Jesus, especially if the one whom we love suffered a long and painful illness before his/her death. The passage, however, wishes to move us deeper than that which appears on the surface. Our union with God does not depend upon a mere identification with the physical suffering that is part of our humanity. Our union with God comes through the gift of God's love, freely bestowed, celebrated by believers in the sacrament of baptism. This free gift of God's love is that which provides the foundation of our hope for life after physical death.

1 JOHN 3:1-2 (790-14/103)

> See what love the Father has given us, that we should be called children of God; and that is what we are. The reason the world does not know us is that it did not know him. Beloved, we are God's children now; what we will be has not yet been revealed. What we do know is this: when he is revealed, we will be like him, for we will see him as he is.

The author declares our status as God's children with alarming simplicity: "that is what we are." No rationale or argumentative proof is given. The fact is simply stated: "we are God's children now."

This being the case, do not hesitate during this time of grief to do what children do when overwhelmed with

fear and doubt. They cry. They call for help. They hold
tightly to the one whose love they know. God gives us
permission to be his children, especially during this time
when we need God's strength and power more than ever
before. Don't be concerned whether the tears, the
complaints, or the "crying out to the Lord" indicates any
lack of faith on our part. It doesn't. It simply acknowl-
edges that we are God's children, very much in need of
comfort and security during a time when everything in
life has shifted. Reflect also on the final line in this
Scripture passage. It reminds us that God cannot (and
will not) deny himself. In other words, God who is Love
cannot deny that he is Love, which means he cannot (and
will not) deny us the love we need now more than ever.

1 JOHN 3:14-16 (790-15/104)

> We know that we have passed from death to life because
> we love one another. Whoever does not love abides in
> death. All who hate a brother or sister are murderers, and
> you know that murderers do not have eternal life abiding
> in them. We know love by this, that he laid down his life
> for us—and we ought to lay down our lives for one
> another.

Love is always life-giving. We have encountered this
truth again and again in the ordinary, everyday experiences of our life. For example, the times that your child
came to you, dried tears staining his/her face, as he/she
held a scraped elbow or cut finger. Recall how you
lovingly wiped away the tears and cleaned the wound,
gently kissing it to "make it better." More than likely,

your child experienced comfort and consolation because your love was life-giving. Your love made it better. If such a transformation and healing can take place because of our human offering of love, how much more will this be true because of God's divine gift of love? The Scripture author does not describe such love as a feeling or an intellectual concept, but as a clearly defined action: "We know love by this, that he [Jesus] laid down his life for us." This is the love by which we know that we have passed from death to life.

REVELATION 14:13 (790-16/105)

> And I heard a voice from heaven saying, "Write this: Blessed are the dead who from now on die in the Lord." "Yes," says the Spirit, "they will rest from their labors, for their deeds follow them."

We know that our deeds cannot earn us salvation. The gracious gift of God, celebrated in the sacraments of initiation (baptism, confirmation, and the Eucharist), offers us the grace of salvation. Yet we would be unrealistic believers if we did not hold that God recognizes our good deeds as times in our life when God's grace worked its transforming power, making us more like Jesus. We can take comfort, therefore, in the knowledge that those who have led a good life—those who have tried to embrace God's beatitude lifestyle—will be recognized by the Lord when he calls us home. Given rest from their labors, they will be seen for what they are: God's children who, like Jesus, responded to the Spirit's call to love and cherish those who had been given to their care during their life in this world.

REVELATION 20:11—21:1 (790-17/106)

Then I saw a great white throne and the one who sat on it; the earth and the heaven fled from his presence, and no place was found for them. And I saw the dead, great and small, standing before the throne, and books were opened. Also another book was opened, the book of life. And the dead were judged according to their works, as recorded in the books. And the sea gave up the dead that were in it, Death and Hades gave up the dead that were in them, and all were judged according to what they had done. Then Death and Hades were thrown into the lake of fire. This is the second death, the lake of fire; and anyone whose name was not found written in the book of life was thrown into the lake of fire.

Then I saw a new heaven and a new earth; for the first heaven and the first earth had passed away, and the sea was no more.

There is no doubt within our Christian tradition that we are held accountable for our life here on earth. The author's description indicates this when he says, "And I saw the dead, great and small, standing before the throne, and books were opened." Rather than frightening us with this truth, however, the passage's symbolic and poetic language conveys a sense of hope that our efforts in this life will be rewarded in the life to come. Our God is not a capricious God who arbitrarily punishes and rewards men and women. Our God is the God of love who empowers us to love so we can recognize Love when God calls us home. The good works that frame our lifestyle in this world, therefore, are the reflection of God's grace working in us. As these good works multiply during our human lifetime, we learn to recognize their true source: God's love unfolding within us, drawing others into that embrace.

REVELATION 21:1-5A, 6B-7 (790-18/<u>107</u>)

> Then I saw a new heaven and a new earth; for the first heaven and the first earth had passed away, and the sea was no more. And I saw the holy city, the new Jerusalem, coming down out of heaven from God, prepared as a bride adorned for her husband. And I heard a loud voice from the throne saying,
>
> > "See, the home of God is among mortals.
> > He will dwell with them as their God;
> > they will be his peoples,
> > and God himself will be with them;
> > he will wipe every tear from their eyes.
> > Death will be no more;
> > mourning and crying and pain will be no more,
> > for the first things have passed away."
>
> > And the one who was seated on the throne said, "See, I am making all things new. I am the Alpha and the Omega, the beginning and the end. To the thirsty I will give water as a gift from the spring of the water of life. Those who conquer will inherit these things, and I will be their God and they will be my children."

There are two times when people usually cry in church: weddings and funerals. In both cases there is a sense of finality and a sense of newness. Though happy for their daughter, the bride's parents cry because they experience a type of death: their daughter will no longer be with them in the same way. Likewise, the family and friends of the deceased grieve because their spouse, parent, child, friend, or sibling will no longer be with them in the same way. In both cases, there is the experience of separation and death. In both cases, however, there is also the experience of hope and new beginnings.

The juxtaposition of these two images—a bride "adorned for her husband" with the image of a new world, where "crying and pain will be no more"—can offer us who remain a word of comfort and consolation. This is unveiled in the author's description of that new order. It will be a time of divine presence when "the home of God is among mortals"; a time of intimacy when "God himself will be with them"; a time of consolation and comfort when "he will wipe every tear from their eyes"; a time of healing when "pain will be no more."

The most exciting part of this passage, however, is the ending promise in which God guarantees that "I will be their God and they will be my children." What more could we ask for the person we love so deeply?

RESPONSORIAL PSALMS

PSALM 23 (791-1/<u>108</u>)

R.   The Lord is my shepherd; there is nothing I shall
     want.
     Or:
R.   Though I walk in the valley of darkness, I fear no
     evil, for you are with me.

PSALM 25:6-7, 17-18, 20-21 (791-2/<u>109</u>)

R.   To you, O Lord, I lift my soul.
     Or:
R.   No one who waits for you, O Lord, will ever be put
     to shame.

PSALM 27:1, 4, 7-9, 13-14 (791-3/<u>110</u>)

R.   The Lord is my light and my salvation.
     Or:
R.   I believe that I shall see the good things of the Lord
     in the land of the living.

PSALM 42:2, 3, 5—43:3, 4, 5 (791-4/<u>111</u>)

R.   My soul is thirsting for the living God: when shall I
     see him face to face?

PSALM 63: 2-3, 3-4, 5-6, 8-9 (791-5/<u>112</u>)

R.   My soul is thirsting for you, O Lord my God.

PSALM 103:8, 10, 13-14, 15-16, 17-18 (791-6/113)

R.   The Lord is kind and merciful.
    Or:
R.   The salvation of the just comes from the Lord.

PSALM 116:5-6, 10-11, 15-16 (791-7/114)

R.   I will walk in the presence of the Lord in the land of
    the living.
    Or:
R.   Alleluia.

PSALM 122:1-2, 3-4, 4-5, 6-7, 8-9 (791-8/115)

R.   I rejoiced when I heard them say: let us go to the
    house of the Lord.
    Or:
R.   Let us go rejoicing to the house of the Lord.

PSALM 130:1-2, 3-4, 4-6, 7-8 (791-9/116)

R.   Out of the depths, I cry to you, Lord.
    Or:
R.   I hope in the Lord, I trust in his word.

PSALM 143:1-2, 5-6, 7-8, 10 (791-10/117)

R.   O Lord, hear my prayer.

ALLELUIA VERSES /
VERSES BEFORE THE GOSPEL

MATTHEW 11:25 (792-1/118)

At that time Jesus said, "I thank you, Father, Lord of heaven and earth, because you have hidden these things from the wise and the intelligent and have revealed them to infants."

MATTHEW 25:34 (792-2/119)

Come, you that are blessed by my Father, inherit the kingdom prepared for you from the foundation of the world.

JOHN 3:16 (792-3/120)

For God so loved the world that he gave his only Son, so that everyone who believes in him may not perish but may have eternal life.

JOHN 6:39 (794-4/121)

And this is the will of him who sent me, that I should lose nothing of all that he has given me, but raise it up on the last day.

JOHN 6:40 (795-5/122)

This is indeed the will of my Father, that all who see the Son and believe in him may have eternal life; and I will raise them up on the last day.

JOHN 6:51A

I am the living bread that came down from heaven.
Whoever eats of this bread will live forever.

JOHN 11:25-26 (796-6/123)

I am the resurrection and the life. Those who believe in
me, even though they die, will live, and everyone who
lives and believes in me will never die.

PHILIPPIANS 3:20 (796-7/124)

But our citizenship is in heaven, and it is from there that
we are expecting a Savior, the Lord Jesus Christ.

2 TIMOTHY 2:11B-12A (796-8/125)

If we have died with him, we will also live with him;
if we endure, we will also reign with him.

REVELATION 1:5A, 6B (796-9/126)

Jesus Christ, the faithful witness, the firstborn of the
dead, to him be glory and dominion forever and ever.
Amen.

REVELATION 14:13 (796-10/127)

Blessed are the dead who from now on die in the Lord;
they will rest from their labors, for their deeds follow
them.

GOSPEL READINGS

MATTHEW 5:1-12 (793-1/<u>128</u>)

> When Jesus saw the crowds, he went up the mountain; and after he sat down, his disciples came to him. Then he began to speak, and taught them, saying:
>
> "Blessed are the poor in spirit, for theirs is the kingdom of heaven.
>
> "Blessed are those who mourn, for they will be comforted.
>
> "Blessed are the meek, for they will inherit the earth.
>
> "Blessed are those who hunger and thirst for righteousness, for they will be filled.
>
> "Blessed are the merciful, for they will receive mercy.
>
> "Blessed are the pure in heart, for they will see God.
>
> "Blessed are the peacemakers, for they will be called children of God.
>
> "Blessed are those who are persecuted for righteousness' sake, for theirs is the kingdom of heaven.
>
> "Blessed are you when people revile you and persecute you and utter all kinds of evil against you falsely on my account. Rejoice and be glad, for your reward is great in heaven, for in the same way they persecuted the prophets who were before you."

Possibly one of the most familiar and popular sections in the Bible, the Beatitudes give us a thumbnail sketch of Jesus. Perhaps that is why the passage attracts us. Each Beatitude reminds us of some aspect of Jesus' personality, ministry, or life, while at the same time reminding us of some attribute which characterizes our loved one.

Like a mantra, the word *blessed* repeats again and again, breaking through the wall of grief that surrounds us. It's as if the Scripture text were trying to convince us that the goodness we see in those around us—in particular, the goodness we see in the deceased—is a sign of God's presence and blessing. The "blessing," however, is not the blessing we usually associate with rewards, as if God were rewarding the person who died. Rather the blessing refers to our experience of God's love manifested in and through the deceased. We are the ones who have been blessed because we were loved by one who showed us God's love.

MATTHEW 11:25-30 (793-2/129)

> At that time Jesus said, "I thank you, Father, Lord of heaven and earth, because you have hidden these things from the wise and the intelligent and have revealed them to infants; yes, Father, for such was your gracious will. All things have been handed over to me by my Father; and no one knows the Son except the Father, and no one knows the Father except the Son and anyone to whom the Son chooses to reveal him.
>
> "Come to me, all you that are weary and are carrying heavy burdens, and I will give you rest. Take my yoke upon you, and learn from me; for I am gentle and humble in heart, and you will find rest for your souls. For my yoke is easy, and my burden is light."

Right now the yoke does not seem all that easy, and the burden seems heavier than we can bear. Nonetheless, the Scripture invites us to approach God and present to him the weariness that comes from crying through the night, so we might find rest.

"Come to me, all you that are weary and are carrying heavy burdens." The invitation seems too good to be true, especially now when we feel so abandoned. It certainly goes contrary to our feelings to think that we can pray with Jesus when he thanks the Father for hiding all these things from the learned and revealing them to infants. Yet this passage is meant to contradict what we are feeling, as it calls us to look at God's wisdom over and above human wisdom. In the days of Jesus, infants had no social status whatsoever. They were dependent upon others for survival, as well as for instruction. This passage turns the table, reminding us that in God's plan, infants, that is, those completely dependent upon others, are the very ones to whom God reveals all that is hidden! The passage tries to catch us off guard so we can reevaluate how God is working in our lives. To "the wise and the intelligent" among us, death makes no sense. However, God does not reveal the full nature of death's mystery to those who are wise and intelligent. He communicates it to those who are infants, those who are God's children, those who are willing to trust God's plan as it unfolds in their lives.

In the midst of death, therefore, the Lord calls us to come to him so he might reveal to us, his children, God's incredible plan of eternal life.

MATTHEW 25:1-13 (793-3/130)

> "Then the kingdom of heaven will be like this. Ten
> bridesmaids took their lamps and went to meet the
> bridegroom. Five of them were foolish, and five were
> wise. When the foolish took their lamps, they took no oil
> with them; but the wise took flasks of oil with their
> lamps. As the bridegroom was delayed, all of them
> became drowsy and slept. But at midnight there was a
> shout, 'Look! Here is the bridegroom! Come out to meet
> him.' Then all those bridesmaids got up and trimmed
> their lamps. The foolish said to the wise, 'Give us some
> of your oil, for our lamps are going out.' But the wise
> replied, 'No! there will not be enough for you and for us;
> you had better go to the dealers and buy some for
> yourselves.' And while they went to buy it, the bride-
> groom came, and those who were ready went with him
> into the wedding banquet; and the door was shut. Later
> the other bridesmaids came also, saying, 'Lord, lord,
> open to us.' But he replied, 'Truly I tell you, I do not
> know you.' Keep awake therefore, for you know neither
> the day nor the hour."

For those who remain, death is a very sobering
experience. Confronted by its forced entry into the life of
someone we love, we necessarily confront thoughts of
our own death. Indeed, the mystery of death challenges
us to examine the mystery of life.

Experience has shown that God's grace slips into our
lives between the cracks. Times of stress, when our
human frailty is broken into small pieces that cannot be
reassembled; times of change, when our supposedly
secure foundation is shaken at the core; times of grief,
when the normalcy of our lives is spinning out of control—all of these times are moments of grace, helping us

to view the world with a different set of eyes, and measure what's important with a different set of rulers.

The passage from Matthew is precisely one of those times. Using a parable, Jesus talks about bridesmaids' being ready for the coming of the bridegroom. In the time of Jesus, the bridesmaids were expected to wait outside the bride's house until the groom arrived. It was customary for the bridegroom to "delay" his coming to the very last moment, and then to arrive unexpectedly with his entourage. The bridesmaids were expected to be waiting, lamps trimmed, so they could lead the bridegroom and the guests into the wedding area. Those whose lamps were empty could not be part of the wedding procession, hence the need to be prepared with extra supplies lest the bridegroom be delayed.

So it is true for us. Our bridegroom will indeed come for us. We need to be ready, our life in Christ having stored up treasure in heaven, so we can participate in the eternal wedding feast God prepares for those who await his coming. For the Christian, therefore, the mystery of death reveals the mystery of life.

MATTHEW 25:31-46 (793-4/131)

> "When the Son of Man comes in his glory, and all the angels with him, then he will sit on the throne of his glory. All the nations will be gathered before him, and he will separate people one from another as a shepherd separates the sheep from the goats, and he will put the sheep at his right hand and the goats at the left. Then the king will say to those at his right hand, 'Come, you that are blessed by my Father, inherit the kingdom prepared

for you from the foundation of the world; for I was
hungry and you gave me food, I was thirsty and you gave
me something to drink, I was a stranger and you
welcomed me, I was naked and you gave me clothing, I
was sick and you took care of me, I was in prison and
you visited me.' Then the righteous will answer him,
'Lord, when was it that we saw you hungry and gave you
food, or thirsty and gave you something to drink? And
when was it that we saw you a stranger and welcomed
you, or naked and gave you clothing? And when was it
that we saw you sick or in prison and visited you?' And
the king will answer them, 'Truly I tell you, just as you
did it to one of the least of these who are members of my
family, you did it to me.' Then he will say to those at his
left hand, 'You that are accursed, depart from me into the
eternal fire prepared for the devil and his angels; for I
was hungry and you gave me no food, I was thirsty and
you gave me nothing to drink, I was a stranger and you
did not welcome me, naked and you did not give me
clothing, sick and in prison and you did not visit me.'
Then they also will answer, 'Lord, when was it that we
saw you hungry or thirsty or a stranger or naked or sick
or in prison, and did not take care of you?' Then he will
answer them, 'Truly I tell you, just as you did not do it to
one of the least of these, you did not do it to me.' And
these will go away into eternal punishment, but the
righteous into eternal life."

The meaning of this passage seems pretty straightfor-
ward: we will be judged by the ways we have treated one
another. And on one level, that certainly gives us insight
as to how we are to relate to one another. We are to carry
the love of Jesus to those around us.

On another level, however, God's word asks us to
approach our relationship with one another from a
different angle. Not only are we expected to treat one

another with respect and love, regardless of a person's life situation (hungry, imprisoned, homeless, ill), but we are expected to accept one another as Jesus' emissaries sent to gain our attention and obtain our allegiance to the Lord. During the time of Jesus, emissaries were more than representatives or spokespersons. They were, in a sense, the very presence of the person who had sent them. In this passage, therefore, the poor, the homeless, the sick, and the imprisoned are not just people in need. They are viewed as God's emissaries, God's very presence. Acceptance or rejection of such a person, therefore, was literally the acceptance or rejection of God.

This insight helps us understand how God is everywhere, continually inviting us to love, even in difficult situations. The reason we do so is not just because a person is in need, but because God, in some sense, is also in need through that person. What a great privilege we have been given to satisfy God's needs by tending to the needs of those whom he has sent in his name.

MARK 15:33-39; 16:1-6 (793-5/132)

> When it was noon, darkness came over the whole land until three in the afternoon. At three o'clock Jesus cried out with a loud voice, "Eloi, Eloi, lema sabachthani?" which means, "My God, my God, why have you forsaken me?" When some of the bystanders heard it, they said, "Listen, he is calling for Elijah." And someone ran, filled a sponge with sour wine, put it on a stick, and gave it to him to drink, saying, "Wait, let us see whether Elijah will come to take him down." Then Jesus gave a

loud cry and breathed his last. And the curtain of the
temple was torn in two, from top to bottom. Now when
the centurion, who stood facing him, saw that in this way
he breathed his last, he said, "Truly this man was God's
Son!"

   When the sabbath was over, Mary Magdalene, and
Mary the mother of James, and Salome bought spices, so
that they might go and anoint him. And very early on the
first day of the week, when the sun had risen, they went
to the tomb. They had been saying to one another, "Who
will roll away the stone for us from the entrance to the
tomb?" When they looked up, they saw that the stone,
which was very large, had already been rolled back. As
they entered the tomb, they saw a young man, dressed in
a white robe, sitting on the right side; and they were
alarmed. But he said to them, "Do not be alarmed; you
are looking for Jesus of Nazareth, who was crucified. He
has been raised; he is not here. Look, there is the place
they laid him."

We know all about darkness. Like a damp winter's
cold, we feel it in every part of our body, whether we are
awake or asleep. We want so much to see again some
glimmer of light, to feel again the warmth of God's love.
All our feelings, however, shout forsaken.

   God also experienced such darkness. We often forget
that truth, thinking of Jesus as someone who sailed
through life and death without any feelings whatsoever.
The text from Mark's Gospel tells us otherwise. Jesus,
fully God and fully human, experienced what it means to
feel forsaken, to suffer pain and death, to feel abandoned
and betrayed.

   The author, however, does not leave us on the cross.
Mark begins the next section with the women's exciting

discovery that the tomb was empty: "Do not be alarmed; you are looking for Jesus of Nazareth, who was crucified. He has been raised." The conclusion we are to make is clear: just as Jesus who suffered pain and death was raised from the dead, so will we, and those whom we love, experience resurrection. Although our present reference point is limited to the pain and death that is part of our human life, Christians look with hope to the final part of the human journey, the part which Jesus already experienced, when we too will know the resurrection power of God.

LUKE 7:11-17 (793-6/133)

> Soon afterwards he went to a town called Nain, and his disciples and a large crowd went with him. As he approached the gate of the town, a man who had died was being carried out. He was his mother's only son, and she was a widow; and with her was a large crowd from the town. When the Lord saw her, he had compassion for her and said to her, "Do not weep." Then he came forward and touched the bier, and the bearers stood still. And he said, "Young man, I say to you, rise!" The dead man sat up and began to speak, and Jesus gave him to his mother. Fear seized all of them; and they glorified God, saying, "A great prophet has risen among us!" and "God has looked favorably on his people!" This word about him spread throughout Judea and all the surrounding country.

The Gospel of Luke reveals Jesus as the one who shows compassion, especially toward society's outcasts and women. This is evident from the above text, which poignantly describes the deceased as "his mother's only son, and she was a widow." You can imagine Jesus gently holding the grieving mother in his arms as he offered comfort and consolation. His words, however, take us by surprise: "Do not weep." We know from experience that weeping is an important part of grieving. Jesus' instruction, therefore, goes against current wisdom. Could he be telling the woman not to grieve the loss of his son?

Scripture scholars explain this apparent contradiction by reminding us that Jesus' earthly ministry points to his final ministry of reconciliation when he raises us from the dead. Just as Jesus raised the widow's son from the dead, we can look to the time when Jesus will raise us and our loved ones from the dead. Although we weep now, our tears need not flow forever, for God's compassion will bring to life those who have died, just as God's compassion brought back to life the widow's son.

LUKE 12:35-40 (793-7/134)

"Be dressed for action and have your lamps lit; be like those who are waiting for their master to return from the wedding banquet, so that they may open the door for him as soon as he comes and knocks. Blessed are those slaves whom the master finds alert when he comes; truly I tell you, he will fasten his belt and have them sit down to eat, and he will come and serve them. If he comes during the middle of the night, or near dawn, and finds them so, blessed are those slaves.

"But know this: if the owner of the house had known at what hour the thief was coming, he would not

have let his house be broken into. You also must be
ready, for the Son of Man is coming at an unexpected
hour."

The closest most of us come to seeing a servant in
action is when we attend the movies. There we encounter
a wide variety of servant lifestyles, from the indentured
servants of early America to the professional servants
epitomized by Anthony Hopkins in *Remains of the Day*.
Through the movie's window of escape, we have been
able to peer into a servant's world, learning quite a bit
about their duties. We know, for example, that they help
the master through the day, provide for his/her every
need, come when called, and leave when dismissed. For
that reason, Luke's description of a master's serving the
slave or servant shatters our expectations. The master, of
course, represents God, who comes to us, sometimes
unexpectedly. When we are prepared for his coming, the
unexpected takes place: God serves us! Be consoled
knowing that when we need God most of all, at the time
of death, our God comes as servant, ready to provide for
our needs.

LUKE 23:33, 39-43 (793-8/135)

When they came to the place that is called The Skull,
they crucified Jesus there with the criminals, one on his
right and one on his left.
    One of the criminals who were hanged there kept
deriding him and saying, "Are you not the Messiah?
Save yourself and us!" But the other rebuked him,

saying, "Do you not fear God, since you are under the
same sentence of condemnation? And we indeed have
been condemned justly, for we are getting what we
deserve for our deeds, but this man has done nothing
wrong." Then he said, "Jesus, remember me when you
come into your kingdom." He replied, "Truly I tell you,
today you will be with me in Paradise."

Sometimes we rhapsodize the life of the person who
has died to such a degree that it becomes unrecognizable
to those around. Bereavement counselors tell us that this
is a normal part of the grieving process. The text from
Luke, however, can help the Christian embrace the "good
thief" part of our life, confident that we do not have to
present a sanitized version to God, or, for that matter, to
those around us. God is quite willing to accept us as we
are, despite our sinfulness. Why else would Jesus have
embraced the same death that we embrace, if not to bring
us the hope of eternal life?

LUKE 23:44-46, 50, 52-53; 24:1-5 (793-9/136)

It was now about noon, and darkness came over the
whole land until three in the afternoon, while the sun's
light failed; and the curtain of the temple was torn in
two. Then Jesus, crying with a loud voice, said, "Father,
into your hands I commend my spirit." Having said this,
he breathed his last.
    Now there was a good and righteous man named
Joseph, who, though a member of the council, had not
agreed to their plan and action. This man went to Pilate
and asked for the body of Jesus. Then he took it down,
wrapped it in a linen cloth, and laid it in a rock-hewn
tomb where no one had ever been laid.

> But on the first day of the week, at early dawn, they came to the tomb, taking the spices that they had prepared. They found the stone rolled away from the tomb, but when they went in, they did not find the body. While they were perplexed about this, suddenly two men in dazzling clothes stood beside them. The women were terrified and bowed their faces to the ground, but the men said to them, "Why do you look for the living among the dead? He is not here, but has risen."

Jesus' prayer, "Father, into your hands I commend my spirit," is taken from Psalm 22, the night prayer of the pious Jew, coupled with the "Abba" term of endearment associated with Jesus' intimate relationship with God. Even as he embraced death, Jesus remained rooted in his relationship with the Father, accepting death not as a final end, but the coming of night that precedes the dawn. It is the assurance that death will lead to resurrection, just as night leads to the dawn.

For the Christian, therefore, the night prayer image contained in this passage provides a powerful beacon of hope. Just as we expect the dawn when we prepare ourselves for slumber, so we can expect resurrection as we prepare ourselves for death.

LUKE 24:13-35 (793-10/<u>137</u>)

> Now on that same day two of them were going to a village called Emmaus, about seven miles from Jerusalem, and talking with each other about all these things that had happened. While they were talking and discussing, Jesus himself came near and went with them, but their eyes were kept from recognizing him. And he

said to them, "What are you discussing with each other
while you walk along?" They stood still, looking sad.
Then one of them, whose name was Cleopas, answered
him, "Are you the only stranger in Jerusalem who does
not know the things that have taken place there in these
days?" He asked them, "What things?" They replied,
"The things about Jesus of Nazareth, who was a prophet
mighty in deed and word before God and all the people,
and how our chief priests and leaders handed him over to
be condemned to death and crucified him. But we had
hoped that he was the one to redeem Israel. Yes, and
besides all this, it is now the third day since these things
took place. Moreover, some women of our group
astounded us. They were at the tomb early this morning,
and when they did not find his body there, they came
back and told us that they had indeed seen a vision of
angels who said that he was alive. Some of those who
were with us went to the tomb and found it just as the
women had said; but they did not see him." Then he said
to them, "Oh, how foolish you are, and how slow of
heart to believe all that the prophets have declared! Was
it not necessary that the Messiah should suffer these
things and then enter into his glory?" Then beginning
with Moses and all the prophets, he interpreted to them
the things about himself in all the scriptures.

As they came near the village to which they were
going, he walked ahead as if he were going on. But they
urged him strongly, saying, "Stay with us, because it is
almost evening and the day is now nearly over." So he
went in to stay with them. When he was at the table with
them, he took bread, blessed and broke it, and gave it to
them. Then their eyes were opened, and they recognized
him; and he vanished from their sight. They said to each
other, "Were not our hearts burning within us while he
was talking to us on the road, while he was opening the
scriptures to us?" That same hour they got up and
returned to Jerusalem; and they found the eleven and

their companions gathered together. They were saying,
"The Lord has risen indeed, and he has appeared to
Simon!" Then they told what had happened on the road,
and how he had been made known to them in the
breaking of the bread.

"Then their eyes were opened, and they recognized
him."

The breaking of the bread. The phrase itself suggests
ritual and mystery and sharing and nourishment and
security. For the Christian, the breaking of the bread is
shorthand for the celebration of the Eucharist, the
ritualized sacred meal that nourishes believers through
their sharing in the Body and Blood of Christ. In the
ritual itself, we experience a sense of security, always
knowing where we are in the prayer even when our
attention wanders. The Church teaches that Jesus is in
that meal; that Jesus is in the celebration; that Jesus is
presiding at the table; that Jesus is breaking the bread
with us and for us; that Jesus is that bread.

There are times, however, when life's situations
cloud our eyes, hiding the levels of truth celebrated when
we break the bread with Jesus. More often than not, we
fail to recognize him at these times because we fail to
understand God's plan of salvation. We fail to understand
how suffering and death can be part of God's life-giving
plan for creation. This was true of the disciples on the
road to Emmaus: "Was it not necessary that the Messiah
should suffer these things and then enter into his glory?"
So it is true for us. What finally opened the eyes of the
disciples was their participating in "the breaking of the
bread." And so it will be for us.

JOHN 5:24-29

"Very truly, I tell you, anyone who hears my word and
believes him who sent me has eternal life, and does not
come under judgment, but has passed from death
to life.

"Very truly, I tell you, the hour is coming, and is
now here, when the dead will hear the voice of the Son
of God, and those who hear will live. For just as the
Father has life in himself, so he has granted the Son also
to have life in himself; and he has given him authority to
execute judgment, because he is the Son of Man. Do not
be astonished at this; for the hour is coming when all
who are in their graves will hear his voice and will come
out—those who have done good, to the resurrection of
life, and those who have done evil, to the resurrection of
condemnation."

What Christians believe as true is nothing less than
astonishing: "For the hour is coming when all who are in
their graves will hear his voice and will come out." How
can one believe such a claim? We will come from our
graves! It's preposterous. The whole of the Christian life,
however, revolves around the truth of resurrection.
Without this truth, our faith is useless, our hope for
tomorrow fruitless, our tears of grief endless. If only it
could be proven, one might say. If only we could know
for certain.

The passage from John gives us the way to experience the inner certainty we seek. "Anyone who hears my
word and believes him who sent me has eternal life." To
experience that inner certainty, we need to hear God's
word and believe in the one the Father sent. This requires

effort and discipline on our part. It does not come easy, although the grace is given freely. Hearing God's word in the Scripture by spending time in prayer, and modeling our life on Jesus, the one whom the Father sent, will help us experience that inner certainty. It may not happen quickly, but it will occur as we give God permission to speak his word to us, and give God permission to shape our life according to his Gospel.

JOHN 6:37-40 (793-11/138)

> "Everything that the Father gives me will come to me, and anyone who comes to me I will never drive away; for I have come down from heaven, not to do my own will, but the will of him who sent me. And this is the will of him who sent me, that I should lose nothing of all that he has given me, but raise it up on the last day. This is indeed the will of my Father, that all who see the Son and believe in him may have eternal life; and I will raise them up on the last day."

Jesus came to fulfill the Father's plan. How comforting to know that God's plan will not be foiled, that "anyone who comes to me I will never drive away." Unfortunately, we often limit God's plan by thinking that our sin cannot be overcome by his mercy. Yet John's Gospel reminds us that Jesus will "lose nothing of all that he [the Father] has given me." Jesus came to make sure that nothing and no one is lost as the Father's plan unfolds, transforming our experience of death into his experience of everlasting life.

JOHN 6:51-58 (793-12/<u>139</u>)

> "I am the living bread that came down from heaven. Whoever eats of this bread will live forever; and the bread that I will give for the life of the world is my flesh."
>
> The Jews then disputed among themselves, saying, "How can this man give us his flesh to eat?" So Jesus said to them, "Very truly, I tell you, unless you eat the flesh of the Son of Man and drink his blood, you have no life in you. Those who eat my flesh and drink my blood have eternal life, and I will raise them up on the last day; for my flesh is true food and my blood is true drink. Those who eat my flesh and drink my blood abide in me, and I in them. Just as the living Father sent me, and I live because of the Father, so whoever eats me will live because of me. This is the bread that came down from heaven, not like that which your ancestors ate, and they died. But the one who eats this bread will live forever."

John's Gospel provides us with the famous Bread of Life passages which have shaped the Catholic community's understanding of the Eucharist. We know that our journey of faith begins with baptism, continuing through the remaining sacraments of initiation, confirmation, and the Eucharist. It is our ongoing participation in and celebration of the Eucharist that strengthens us as we journey to the Father. St. Ignatius calls it the "medicine of immortality," since the reception of the Eucharist carries with it Jesus' promise: "The one who eats this bread will live forever." Reception of the Eucharist, therefore, sustains the new life given us in baptism, preserving us through physical death for the life that is eternal.

During the time of grieving, participation in the Eucharist, therefore, will be a source of comfort and grace. The Lord will use this "medicine of immortality" to heal our own wounds, caused by the death of the one we love. Unfortunately, some people stay away from the Eucharist during this time, their feelings of anger toward God convincing them that they do not belong there. If you find yourself in that position, remember Jesus' words: "I am the living bread that came down from heaven." This is the bread we need more than ever when we have been depleted by the pain of grief. Take and eat what is offered.

JOHN 11:17-27 (793-13/<u>140</u>)

> When Jesus arrived, he found that Lazarus had already been in the tomb four days. Now Bethany was near Jerusalem, some two miles away, and many of the Jews had come to Martha and Mary to console them about their brother. When Martha heard that Jesus was coming, she went and met him, while Mary stayed at home. Martha said to Jesus, "Lord, if you had been here, my brother would not have died. But even now I know that God will give you whatever you ask of him." Jesus said to her, "Your brother will rise again." Martha said to him, "I know that he will rise again in the resurrection on the last day." Jesus said to her, "I am the resurrection and the life. Those who believe in me, even though they die, will live, and everyone who lives and believes in me will never die. Do you believe this?" She said to him, "Yes, Lord, I believe that you are the Messiah, the Son of God, the one coming into the world."

We easily identify with Martha's complaint. Like us, both Martha and Mary had sent word to Jesus that their brother was dying. Despite their plea begging him to come, Jesus failed to arrive until Lazarus had been in the tomb four days. How fervently we also begged Jesus to hear our prayer for our beloved, yet Jesus failed to come. Perhaps we had prayed for additional time so we could express our love or ask for forgiveness; perhaps we prayed that our loved one regain consciousness so he/she could speak one last word to the family; perhaps we implored God to be merciful and extend his healing power, restoring our loved one to health. But he did not come. We were forced to give back to God the one we love, just as Martha and Mary were forced to give Lazarus back to God.

Martha continues her complaint: "Lord, if you had been here, my brother would not have died." Although the text presents her words as a statement of faith, "But even now I know that God will give you whatever you ask of him," I believe that Martha hurled the words at Jesus not even trying to hide her anger. Yet, Jesus took her as she was, filled with frustration, grief, and anger, and asked her to take another step with him. "Your brother will rise again," Jesus tells her, to which Martha replies in the affirmative: "I know that he will rise again in the resurrection on the last day." Like us, Martha believed in the resurrection intellectually. That, however, did not take away the pain and the grief that filled her heart. Nevertheless, Jesus pursues her, not wishing her to remain short of the goal. He tells her, "I am the resurrection and the life. . . . Do you believe this?"

Was Martha's response a resounding, "Yes, Lord, I believe," spoken with an unwavering voice and head held high? I don't think so. Her response probably resembled a whimper or sob, barely audible through the tears: "Yes, Lord, I believe." It was that whispered, tear-laden cry of belief that was accepted by Jesus.

As Jesus accepted Martha's response, be confident he will accept ours.

JOHN 11:32-45 (793-14/141)

> When Mary came where Jesus was and saw him, she knelt at his feet and said to him, "Lord, if you had been here, my brother would not have died." When Jesus saw her weeping, and the Jews who came with her also weeping, he was greatly disturbed in spirit and deeply moved. He said, "Where have you laid him?" They said to him, "Lord, come and see." Jesus began to weep. So the Jews said, "See how he loved him!" But some of them said, "Could not he who opened the eyes of the blind man have kept this man from dying?"
>
> Then Jesus, again greatly disturbed, came to the tomb. It was a cave, and a stone was lying against it. Jesus said, "Take away the stone." Martha, the sister of the dead man, said to him, "Lord, already there is a stench because he has been dead four days." Jesus said to her, "Did I not tell you that if you believed, you would see the glory of God?" So they took away the stone. And Jesus looked upward and said, "Father, I thank you for having heard me. I knew that you always hear me, but I have said this for the sake of the crowd standing here, so that they may believe that you sent me." When he had said this, he cried with a loud voice, "Lazarus, come out!" The dead man came out, his hands and feet bound

with strips of cloth, and his face wrapped in a cloth.
Jesus said to them, "Unbind him, and let him go."

Many of the Jews therefore, who had come with
Mary and had seen what Jesus did, believed in him.

"Unbind him, and let him go." We know that death
unbinds us from this earthly existence, freeing us to enter
fully and deeply into the eternal love of God's Holy
Spirit. No longer bound by sickness or pain, no longer
bound by sin or human limitation, we begin to experience
the greater measure of freedom given God's sons and
daughters. God offers this as a preliminary taste of the
resurrection life that is yet to come.

There is another aspect of unbinding, however, that
needs to be addressed. We ourselves are called to "unbind" the deceased by giving them permission to enter
into the Spirit's loving embrace. In other words, it is
important for us to "let go," not of our memories, but of
our dependence upon the deceased. Although burying
someone we love is difficult, it can be an opportunity to
experience a renewal of grace as we reestablish our
dependence upon the Lord.

JOHN 12:23-28 (793-15/142)

Jesus answered them, "The hour has come for the Son of
Man to be glorified. Very truly, I tell you, unless a grain
of wheat falls into the earth and dies, it remains just a
single grain; but if it dies, it bears much fruit. Those who
love their life lose it, and those who hate their life in this
world will keep it for eternal life. Whoever serves me
must follow me, and where I am, there will my servant
be also. Whoever serves me, the Father will honor.

"Now my soul is troubled. And what should I say—
'Father, save me from this hour'? No, it is for this reason
that I have come to this hour. Father, glorify your name."
Then a voice came from heaven, "I have glorified it, and
I will glorify it again."

From the moment of our baptism, the daily dying to
self acquires new meaning for believers. Baptism
incorporates us into the ongoing process of dying and
rising that is part of God's plan for all creation. The plan
is expressed graphically in the Scripture verse from
John's Gospel: "Unless a grain of wheat falls into the
earth and dies, it remains just a single grain; but if it dies,
it bears much fruit." Without the dying there is no rising.
This occurs not once, but again and again throughout our
daily life. The final death, therefore, comes so we can
rise in glory. It is part of the plan, ordained by God and
embraced by God's Son in his own dying and rising.
Take heart that one has gone ahead of us to show us the
way. Take heart that one has gone ahead of us to show us
the truth that the dying brings the rising.

JOHN 14:1-6 (793-16/143)

"Do not let your hearts be troubled. Believe in God,
believe also in me. In my Father's house there are many
dwelling places. If it were not so, would I have told you
that I go to prepare a place for you? And if I go and
prepare a place for you, I will come again and will take
you to myself, so that where I am, there you may be also.
And you know the way to the place where I am going."
Thomas said to him, "Lord, we do not know where you
are going. How can we know the way?" Jesus said to

him, "I am the way, and the truth, and the life. No one
comes to the Father except through me."

In our tradition, the phrase, "in my Father's house,"
refers to heaven, where God dwells in all, and all dwell in
God. This dwelling place is not meant to suggest a
physical dwelling, but the inexpressible presence of God.
We begin to dwell in this presence, as God's presence
dwells in us, through the power of the Spirit, when we
are made temples of the Holy Spirit in baptism. At the
coming of the Lord, however, God completes the process
"so that where I [Jesus] am, there you may be also."

Especially comforting is Jesus' promise "that I go to
prepare a place for you." Knowing that the Lord already
decided to bring us into his presence and bring God's
presence into our lives is very reassuring. As we remember those who have died, therefore, remember that God
already decided to bring him/her into the Lord's presence. The room is ready.

JOHN 17:24-26 (793-17/144)

"Father, I desire that those also, whom you have given
me, may be with me where I am, to see my glory, which
you have given me because you loved me before the
foundation of the world.

"Righteous Father, the world does not know you,
but I know you; and these know that you have sent me. I
made your name known to them, and I will make it
known, so that the love with which you have loved me
may be in them, and I in them."

We know that God is *Abba*, Father, because Jesus has revealed it to us: "I made your name known to them." Knowing God's name places God in our debt. Now God must be what the name indicates: God is *Abba*, the intimate, passionate presence of Love. Jesus explains the reason he has revealed God's name when he says, "I will make it known, so that the love with which you have loved me may be in them, and I in them." Unbelievable. The very same love that Jesus experienced from *Abba* God is the love we will experience because Jesus revealed God's name to us. That love raised Jesus from the dead. That very same love will raise us also.

JOHN 19:17-18, 25-30

Carrying the cross by himself, [Jesus] went out to what is called The Place of the Skull, which in Hebrew is called Golgotha. There they crucified him, and with him two others, one on either side, with Jesus between them.

And that is what the soldiers did. Meanwhile, standing near the cross of Jesus were his mother, and his mother's sister, Mary the wife of Clopas, and Mary Magdalene. When Jesus saw his mother and the disciple whom he loved standing beside her, he said to his mother, "Woman, here is your son." Then he said to the disciple, "Here is your mother." And from that hour the disciple took her into his own home.

After this, when Jesus knew that all was now finished, he said (in order to fulfill the scripture), "I am thirsty." A jar full of sour wine was standing there. So they put a sponge full of the wine on a branch of hyssop and held it to his mouth. When Jesus had received the wine, he said, "It is finished." Then he bowed his head and gave up his spirit.

When Jesus died on the cross, he gave us two gifts. The primary gift was the gift of the Spirit, given as a guarantee of eternal life: "He bowed his head and gave up his spirit." The second gift was the gift of Mary, his mother, given as a sign of what God will do when we give the Spirit permission to work in our life.

As we struggle through grief, it will be helpful to ask for Mary's help and guidance. Take her into your heart and home, asking her to show you how the Spirit will work during this time of uncertainty and turmoil. Did she not experience the confusion of Jesus' crucifixion? Did she not experience the pain of giving her son back to God? Did she not wonder how God's plan would work in her life, from the moment she heard the angel's greeting? Mary will be a comfort during this time, plus an example. As we speak with her in prayer, she will show us how the Spirit's power will get us through the day—and the night. The disciple whom Jesus loved saw the importance of this second gift and "took her into his own home." Do likewise and experience peace.

READINGS APPROPRIATE FOR CHILDREN'S FUNERALS

Although any Scripture passage may be used during a funeral liturgy, certain readings may be more appropriate when offering a child back to God. In addition to listing some new selections, I have also listed several shorter versions of passages already cited. Reflections on texts that appear elsewhere have been duly noted.

FROM THE OLD TESTAMENT

ISAIAH 25:6A, 7-8A (799-1/203)

> On this mountain the Lord of hosts will make for all
>   peoples
>   a feast of rich food, a feast of well-aged wines.
> And he will destroy on this mountain
>   the shroud that is cast over all peoples,
>   the sheet that is spread over all nations;
>   he will swallow up death forever.
> Then the Lord God will wipe away the tears from all
>   faces.

See Reflection on Isaiah 25:6a, 7-9

LAMENTATIONS 3:22-26 (204)

> The steadfast love of the Lord never ceases,
>   his mercies never come to an end;
> they are new every morning;
>   great is your faithfulness.
> "The Lord is my portion," says my soul,

"therefore I will hope in him."
The Lord is good to those who wait for him,
    to the soul that seeks him.
It is good that one should wait quietly
    for the salvation of the Lord.

See Reflection on Lamentations 3:17-26

FROM THE NEW TESTAMENT

ROMANS 6:3-4, 8-9 (795-1/<u>205</u>)

Do you not know that all of us who have been baptized
into Christ Jesus were baptized into his death? Therefore
we have been buried with him by baptism into death, so
that, just as Christ was raised from the dead by the glory
of the Father, so we too might walk in newness of life.

But if we have died with Christ, we believe that we
will also live with him. We know that Christ, being
raised from the dead, will never die again; death no
longer has dominion over him.

See Reflection on Romans 6:3-9

ROMANS 14:7-9 (795-2/<u>206</u>)

We do not live to ourselves, and we do not die to
ourselves. If we live, we live to the Lord, and if we die,
we die to the Lord; so then, whether we live or whether
we die, we are the Lord's. For to this end Christ died and
lived again, so that he might be Lord of both the dead
and the living.

See Reflection on Romans 14:7-9, 10b-12

1 CORINTHIANS 15:20-23 (795-3/<u>207</u>)

> But in fact Christ has been raised from the dead, the first
> fruits of those who have died. For since death came
> through a human being, the resurrection of the dead has
> also come through a human being; for as all die in Adam,
> so all will be made alive in Christ. But each in his own
> order: Christ the first fruits, then at his coming those who
> belong to Christ.

See Reflection on 1 Corinthians 15:20-24a, 25-28

EPHESIANS 1:3-5 (795-4/<u>208</u>)

> Blessed be the God and Father of our Lord Jesus Christ,
> who has blessed us in Christ with every spiritual blessing
> in the heavenly places, just as he chose us in Christ
> before the foundation of the world to be holy and
> blameless before him in love. He destined us for
> adoption as his children through Jesus Christ, according
> to the good pleasure of his will.

People tell us that we have an angel in heaven. The
words offer little comfort, however, because we want our
angel here. We know all about belonging to God, and
how everyone has to die. But right now, it all seems
empty and cruel. We can believe in our mind that God
"chose us in Christ before the foundation of the world to
be holy and blameless before him in love," but that does
very little to ease the pain of the present moment. We
don't particularly care about being "holy and blameless
before him in love" right now. All we care about is the
pain and the loss and the guilt and the questions and the
whys that have no answer.

Regardless of the feelings right now, we can be certain of one thing. The child we have given back to God is God's child also: "He destined us for adoption as his children through Jesus Christ." And so our child has two parents: we who remember in love, and One who is his/her love forever.

1 THESSALONIANS 4:13-14, 18 (795-5/209)

But we do not want you to be uninformed, brothers and sisters, about those who have died, so that you may not grieve as others do who have no hope. For since we believe that Jesus died and rose again, even so, through Jesus, God will bring with him those who have died. Therefore encourage one another with these words.

See Reflection on 1 Thessalonians 4:13-18

REVELATION 7:9-10, 15-17 (795-6/210)

After this I looked, and there was a great multitude that no one could count, from every nation, from all tribes and peoples and languages, standing before the throne and before the Lamb, robed in white, with palm branches in their hands.They cried out in a loud voice, saying,
"Salvation belongs to our God who is seated on
the throne, and to the Lamb!"
For this reason they are before the throne of God,
and worship him day and night within
his temple,
and the one who is seated on the throne will
shelter them.
They will hunger no more, and thirst no more;
the sun will not strike them,
nor any scorching heat;

> for the Lamb at the center of the throne will be
>   their shepherd,
>   and he will guide them to springs of the
>   water of life,
> and God will wipe away every tear from
>   their eyes."

How do you bury a child? It's out of order. Children bury their parents; parents are never meant to bury their child. The contradiction cannot be resolved easily. So we turn to the Scripture. There we find another contradiction: "The Lamb at the center of the throne will be their shepherd." How can a Lamb be a shepherd? How can a lamb be a guide?

Sometimes God works through contradictions in order to guide us "to springs of the water of life." Burying a child is one of those contradictions. It has no answer other than our hope that one day "God will wipe away every tear."

REVELATION 21:1, 3-5A (795-7/<u>211</u>)

Then I saw a new heaven and a new earth; for the first heaven and the first earth had passed away, and the sea was no more. And I heard a loud voice from the throne saying,

> "See, the home of God is among mortals.
> He will dwell with them as their God;
> they will be his peoples,
> and God himself will be with them;
> he will wipe every tear from their eyes.
> Death will be no more;
> mourning and crying and pain will be no more,
> for the first things have passed away."

> And the one who was seated on the throne said,
> "See, I am making all things new."

"See, I am making all things new." The phrase seems to mock us during this time of grief. The newness was there when our child was alive. Now all is gone, except the tears.

The promise, however, remains: "Death will be no more." Right now it appears too late for such a promise, but the promise remains nonetheless, "Death will be no more." How we want to believe in that promise! How we ache in every part of our being, wanting to believe. But we can't, right now. All we can do is grieve, hoping for the day when "mourning and crying and pain will be no more."

During this time, be certain of this: God is grieving with us.

GOSPEL SELECTIONS

MARK 10:13-16

> People were bringing little children to him in order that he might touch them; and the disciples spoke sternly to them. But when Jesus saw this, he was indignant and said to them, "Let the little children come to me; do not stop them; for it is to such as these that the kingdom of God belongs. Truly I tell you, whoever does not receive the kingdom of God as a little child will never enter it." And he took them up in his arms, laid his hands on them, and blessed them.

Whether our child is old or young, we never want to give him/her up. The image of Jesus taking the children into his arms, therefore, may not offer us much comfort. We don't want him to take our child if it means taking our child away.

Despite our feelings, however, this particular passage can offer us a great deal of hope. Note what it states: "For it is to such as these that the kingdom of God belongs." Although Scripture scholars might offer a different interpretation, we know that God's word speaks to us in our present personal situation. One might take this passage, therefore, as a type of guarantee. God's kingdom belongs to the children. Although separated from us at this time, we have the assurance that theirs is the kingdom of heaven. Faith tells us that we will be together again in that kingdom. Until then we need to keep repeating the promise: "For it is to such as these that the kingdom of God belongs."

JOHN 6:37-39 (220)

"Everything that the Father gives me will come to me, and anyone who comes to me I will never drive away; for I have come down from heaven, not to do my own will, but the will of him who sent me. And this is the will of him who sent me, that I should lose nothing of all that he has given me, but raise it up on the last day."

See Reflection on John 6:37-40

JOHN 6:51-58 (798-3/<u>221</u>)

"I am the living bread that came down from heaven.
Whoever eats of this bread will live forever; and the
bread that I will give for the life of the world is my
flesh."

The Jews then disputed among themselves, saying,
"How can this man give us his flesh to eat?" So Jesus
said to them, "Very truly, I tell you, unless you eat the
flesh of the Son of Man and drink his blood, you have no
life in you. Those who eat my flesh and drink my blood
have eternal life, and I will raise them up on the last day;
for my flesh is true food and my blood is true drink.
Those who eat my flesh and drink my blood abide in me,
and I in them. Just as the living Father sent me, and I live
because of the Father, so whoever eats me will live
because of me. This is the bread that came down from
heaven, not like that which your ancestors ate, and they
died. But the one who eats this bread will live forever."

See Reflection on John 6:51-58

JOHN 11:32-38, 40 (798-4/<u>222</u>)

When Mary came where Jesus was and saw him, she
knelt at his feet and said to him, "Lord, if you had been
here, my brother would not have died." When Jesus saw
her weeping, and the Jews who came with her also
weeping, he was greatly disturbed in spirit and deeply
moved. He said, "Where have you laid him?" They said
to him, "Lord, come and see." Jesus began to weep. So
the Jews said, "See how he loved him!" But some of
them said, "Could not he who opened the eyes of the
blind man have kept this man from dying?"

Then Jesus, again greatly disturbed, came to the
tomb. It was a cave, and a stone was lying against it.

Jesus said to her, "Did I not tell you that if you believed, you would see the glory of God?"

See Reflection on John 11:32-45

JOHN 19:25-30

Standing near the cross of Jesus were his mother, and his mother's sister, Mary the wife of Clopas, and Mary Magdalene. When Jesus saw his mother and the disciple whom he loved standing beside her, he said to his mother, "Woman, here is your son." Then he said to the disciple, "Here is your mother." And from that hour the disciple took her into his own home.

After this, when Jesus knew that all was now finished, he said (in order to fulfill the scripture), "I am thirsty." A jar full of sour wine was standing there. So they put a sponge full of the wine on a branch of hyssop and held it to his mouth. When Jesus had received the wine, he said, "It is finished." Then he bowed his head and gave up his spirit.

See Reflection on John 19:17-18, 25-30

CHAPTER FOUR

THE GRIEVING PROCESS

There can't be any more tears. So many have fallen already. Eyes reddened, lips and throat parched, sudden weight loss in a few short days are all signs of mourning. It drains us, both physically and psychologically, depleting our inner resources and disorientating our mental compass.

During this time we travel a journey that, paradoxically, we make alone and with others. Volumes have been written that give the signposts of this journey, helping us to find reference points and markers so that we do not stray too far from the road to wholeness. Dr. Elisabeth Kübler-Ross, a pioneer in the field of death and dying, has identified some of those markers, indicating how they are a normal part of the process that terminal patients undergo. In fact, she affirms clinically what believers know to be true, namely, that death is the final stage of growth in this life.

We who have lost loved ones can also use these markers to help us on our journey from grief to wholeness. Experience has shown that understanding this process can comfort us as we make the journey. It helps us realize that we are not alone—others have traveled the road before us—while giving us courage to continue onward looking for the next marker or reference point on our journey.

In her seminal work, *On Death and Dying*, Dr. Kübler-Ross indicates that there are five stages that the terminally ill patient undergoes. These stages can apply as well to those who are grieving: denial, anger, bargaining, despair, and acceptance. All those who mourn eventually go through these stages, although they are not neatly divided and often overlap. Nevertheless, the road to wholeness seems to pass these markers at some point. It will be helpful, therefore, to identify these markers while we are on the journey. Speaking to someone about them may be the best way to proceed, in that being our own counselor sometimes places us in an endless loop of misinterpretation. This need not be a professional counselor, unless we find ourselves stuck at one particular stage. Normally, any understanding person who is a good listener, one with whom we can share our feelings without fear of rejection, can help us move toward wholeness. Very often those who have experienced a similar loss, e.g., death of a spouse or child, are ideal persons to help us during this time.

THE FIVE STAGES OF GRIEVING

Grief is like a raw, open wound, most often deeper than it appears from the outside. If we tend carefully to that wound, it will heal eventually, although there will always remain a scar reminding us of the healing process that took place. Although we may never get over the loss

of our loved one, we will get better in time—helped by
our memories of the deceased, as we allow our feelings
to surface over a period of time, striving not to suppress
them in an unhealthy fashion. Throughout the process, it
is important that we hold on to hope. Finding people to
listen helps the process proceed, so do not hesitate to join
a support group or be afraid of the feelings that surface.

Although everyone goes through the process in their
own way, all seem to pass through the following stages as
part of the grief process.

DENIAL

> Everyone agreed it was a tragedy. It always is when
> someone is young. I knelt before the casket and offered a
> short prayer before I turned to speak with the mother. I
> could see from her eyes that she barely realized I was
> there. Shrouded in a cloak of silence, she could not even
> nod her head to my words. For her, it had not happened.
> Her child would be home momentarily. After all, she had
> just spoken to him on the phone when he called from the
> rest stop on the turnpike. He would be home momen-
> tarily.

Our first reaction is disbelief. How and why did this
happen to me? Isolation and disorientation overtake us. A
new role has suddenly been thrust upon us: widow,
widower, orphan, only living child, etc. We do not know
where to turn. We erect a wall of silence or a screen of
hysteria to keep the information from sinking into our
consciousness. We remain numb, unable to think clearly,
barely hearing the words of condolences and sympathy
offered by others. The emptiness and darkness seem
unbearable.

ANGER

> Her husband, still as stone, sat next to her. He was a big
> man whose body could not conceal the cauldron inside.
> His youngest son, gone. The son with whom he fished
> and hunted. The son who held such promise. The son
> that reminded him so much of himself as a young man.
> The medic team said there was nothing they could do.
> Death was instantaneous. How could they know? They
> weren't there. Why weren't they there? It was a major
> highway, for God's sake, with cars all over the place.
> Why didn't someone call in the accident sooner?
> Everyone has a cell phone nowadays. Why did it take so
> long? If only they had gotten there sooner.

During this time, we often lash out at God or at
doctors as a way of entering into some type of catharsis
and purging. "It was unfair," "Where was God when I
needed him?", "What kind of God would take my
child?", "Why weren't the doctors more attentive?" etc.
Often this stage includes times of guilt precisely because
we do not think we can or should be angry at God. (It is
good to know, however, that our God is quite capable of
handling our anger, and evidently expects it to happen
since God was the one who created us to go through
these various stages of grieving.) What is most important
during this time is that we try to listen to family and
friends as they assure us that our anger is okay.

BARGAINING

> Members of the community expressed concern. Mary
> was not responding to anyone's overtures of friendship
> and comfort. She isolated herself from the altar guild,

and hadn't shown up for the weekly novena that had
been such an important part of her spiritual life. I made a
pastoral visit the next day, inviting myself over for a cup
of tea. During that time, Mary began to share some of
her fears. She knew that her son, Brian, had not been
attending mass for more than a year. Now she was afraid
that God had condemned him to hell. Needing some
assurance that her son was "safe," she went with her
friend to a psychic who advertised in the local paper. She
was afraid to tell her husband since the sessions cost
more than they could afford, but she wanted to be certain
that her son was okay. Mary experienced a brief time of
comfort from her visit, but now feels a need to return for
another session. She does not know where she will get
the money, but knows that she has more questions that
need answers.

In this phase we relive the anger stage from a
different tack. We bargain with God, asking God to give
us some type of sign—e.g., that the person is at peace, or
that the person forgives us for a past hurt—as a prerequi-
site for getting on with life. At this stage we are vulnerable to pious solutions that can hamper the healing
process (for example, "I saw the image in the photograph
smiling at me"), as well as questionable or dangerous
answers to our questions (for example, "I went to a
psychic who told me that Bob was very happy. I felt very
relieved, so I made a second appointment to see if Bob
wanted anything else").

DESPAIR

I was surprised when Harry walked in. Although his wife
had been an active member of our parish, Harry seldom

accompanied her. I could not imagine what he was going through. Losing a son seems more than a person should be asked to bear. A big man physically, it appeared, at first glance, that grief had worn him down beyond recognition. Although his size was the same, his demeanor and stance looked hollow and fragile as he stood in the doorway.

It didn't take long to realize that Harry's bottled anger had eaten his inner core of self-worth and integrity. He saw himself as nothing—useless, estranged from the woman he loved—sinking fast into the depths of self-pity. "Why didn't I let him stay overnight at his friend's house?" he asked me. "Why did I insist that he help me work on the roof early in the morning? It could have waited. If I had waited, he'd be here." The sobs were uncontrollable. I had no answers, and could only hold him tightly to my chest.

Depression, often associated with self-anger, can begin to wear us down at this time. The reality has sunk in, although it is not yet integrated into our life. The future that looms ahead of us seems more than we can handle. We tend to turn in on ourselves, losing any desire to continue with our life. There are many moments during which we second-guess or blame ourselves—that is, "if only I had . . ." or "I should have done such and such." During this stage very little comforts us. If friends and family are present at this time, and are willing to stand by us in silence, offering the comfort of an embrace and the assurance of a gentle touch, we will find our way through.

ACCEPTANCE

Harry accepted my offer to meet weekly for an after-
dinner cup of coffee and piece of cake at the rectory. For
more than a year we discussed a lot of topics, many of
which included reminiscences of his son. I really saw
God's grace working when he asked me to join him and
his wife for dinner at their house. It gave us a chance to
review all that had happened over the year. Mary
acknowledged that she was a bit jealous that someone
had taken an interest in her husband when she was the
active parishioner. It was only later, she said, that she
realized how many people had been trying to reach out to
her from the very first moment, but she had blocked
them out. Once she became aware of this, she was able
to respond more positively to her friends' genuine
concern.

Of special help was an older couple in the parish
whose house she cleaned. They were able to share their
own grief at losing a daughter more than forty years ago.
They showed her that grieving does not mean forgetting,
but remembering that life must continue if we are to hold
the deceased lovingly in our hearts. Harry talked about
his need to love Mary in a physical way, and how
difficult it was for her to respond to him. Luckily Harry's
hunting partner, a professional counselor, was able to
advise him in this area, thus avoiding an irreparable
breakup with the wife he adored. They confided in me
that they were able to dismantle their son's room only
recently. "Perhaps it should have happened sooner,"
Harry said, "but we had to do it in our own time. It was
hard, but we knew that the time had finally come."

Acceptance does not mean that we forget our loss.
On the contrary, it means that we are willing to live with
our loss in a healthy way, namely, by accepting the reality
that our loved one is no longer with us, and that we can

continue. During this stage we begin to understand that
we are now able to relate to the deceased in a different
way, through our relationship with Jesus. Faith is critical
in this stage. Our belief in the communion of saints and
in the resurrection can be a tremendous source of grace
for us, enabling us to accept the paschal mystery in our
own life: accepting the dying experience as we look
toward the rising experience exemplified in Jesus,
the Lord.

HOW DO WE COPE?

The baby's cry remained unanswered—indeed, to all
appearances, unnoticed by the baby's mother, Dee.
Craig, the husband, had just returned from work. Hearing
the baby's crying, he went over, picked up the child, and
cradled her in his arms. She had to be changed. How
long had his precious daughter remained in this condi-
tion, he wondered. He went to the nursery to take care of
the baby. Upon arriving, all he could do was sob. Would
things ever return to normal? Would his wife ever
recover from her dad's prolonged illness and eventual
death? Shouldn't she be back on track by now?

Grieving is hard work because it involves a reorien-
tation of our expectations and activities. We are immobilized by a lack of energy; uncomfortable in ordinary
situations; worn out by infections, colds, loss of appetite;
and turned inward because of fear, anxiety, and what we
perceive to be a loss of faith. All this takes its toll,
depleting our physical and mental stamina, causing lack
of patience and unexplained irritability. All in all, we are
simply not ourselves for ourselves or towards others.

This exasperates the situation even further. We think we should be "doing better," yet find that we can't. We even get angry at ourselves for feeling the way we do when we want to be stronger—especially when we are concerned about other family members.

We forget that grief takes place because we love. Although the intensity of grief is not necessarily determined by the intensity of love, grief occurs because of love. Since we were vulnerable in the relationship with our loved one (vulnerability being an essential part of love), we experience hurt, that is, grief, when the one whom we shared life with, and gave life to, and lived life for, is no longer with us. Since loving involves vulnerability, we now hurt (grieve) because of love, since the one we loved has died and is no longer part of our life as he/she was before. We are, in short, hurt by loving, and so we grieve.

Coping with these feelings is part of the hard work of grieving. It involves a willingness to face the reality in which we find ourselves. This, of course, is both difficult and painful. Seldom do we remember that the pain of grieving can be healthy, one that will heal us as we let the process unfold. More than likely, we try to ignore or cover it, rather than acknowledge and embrace it. Going through the stages listed above is part of the process that leads us to face the reality of our loss. Failure to grieve these losses, however, fills us with fear to love or risk love again.

> She always thought they'd grow old together. It never entered her mind that one day she would be a young widow, confused by a pending negligence lawsuit, overwhelmed by people's advice on how to continue her

life, and so totally alone at the time of her life when she needed desperately to hold tightly to someone. She had loved her husband more than words could say. He was her best friend, her lover, her confidant. Now she had nothing. Even her friends had abandoned her, thinking that she should "get on with life." How could they understand? They never had what she and Bob had. Their ten-year marriage had been a joyful experience of mutual fulfillment. She would never let him go, even though he was gone. How could she? Why should she?

We need also to move on without the bonds of the past holding us back. This corresponds to Dr. Kübler-Ross's fourth stage of despair, in which we cannot imagine the future without the presence of our loved one. Yet a necessary part of the grieving process is precisely our ability to imagine the future, and in imagining the future, to proceed in that direction, no longer held bound by past wishes and dreams—e.g., the retirement vacation you had planned, your child's graduation ceremony you had anticipated, the support of a spouse to bring up the set of twins that were just born, etc. At this point it is important for us to leave behind any guilt we feel—e.g., children feeling they were guilty for a parent's death, a widower feeling guilty that he didn't call 911 quickly enough, etc.

Sometimes people remain fixed at this stage, continually trying to shed the layer of guilt that covers them. They try to do this by thinking that a type of restitution will make it all better—for example, buying a big memorial stone. Such an approach does not help us move ahead, but keeps us on a constant treadmill of trying to achieve some form of restitution that salves our heart. Some form of counseling is often helpful at this time, although family and friends can be of great assistance by helping those who mourn face their limitations in the present situation.

> I can never thank the bereavement team for all they did for me. Unable to speak with my siblings, I found God's grace in the small bereavement group that met in the rectory basement every Tuesday night. Who would have thought that speaking with strangers could be such a help. Of course, they're not strangers now. They're soul mates. They understood me when I didn't understand myself! I would never have had the courage to continue without them. Everyone else was telling me I had to "move on" with my life. The group never told me to do anything. They simply took my hand and my heart and walked with me, showing me ever so gently that I really had loved my spouse to the point of death, and that nothing more was required.

The final stage is acceptance, when we begin to develop new hopes and new dreams while lovingly and gently treasuring past memories. At this point, we have learned how to be patient with ourselves. Community— be it family, neighbors, or church—can be a healing presence for those who mourn in that it provides the necessary channels for new hopes and new dreams to become a reality for those who have lost a loved one.

COMMUNICATION IS THERAPEUTIC

The grieving process reaches an impasse when honest communication breaks down—when we fail to identify in an honest, self-reflective manner our own inner feelings and emotions, and/or share our feelings with others. This inevitably leads to misunderstandings, alienation, isolation, loneliness, and discord among and between family and friends. Shakespeare's *Macbeth* reminds us, "Give sorrow words. The grief that does not speak whispers the o'erfraught heart and bids it break."

Married couples need to be especially sensitive in this area since each partner grieves according to a unique time table and each may have opposite needs in terms of the grieving process. Keeping lines of communication open, making individual needs known to the other, become very important lest one partner inadvertently hurt the other through an insensitive remark or gesture or statement. This is especially true when the loss involves a child.

HOW DO CHILDREN COPE?

Tragedy does not respect age. We sometimes forget that children also need to go through the grieving process lest their life short-circuit, causing difficulties as they approach adulthood. What is important in helping a child through this process is to realize that children process the information and express themselves differently than adults. For that reason we have to use a different set of helping hands as we assist a child through the grieving process.

A main ingredient in this process is our willingness to listen, not just with our ears but with our heart and our senses. Look at the child's actions: the games played, the drawings colored, the gestures made. Avoid surrounding the child with silence, thinking that you're giving the child an opportunity to get in touch with his/her feelings. A child should not be left to deal with grief alone. This does not mean that we constantly badger the child with questions or probe into his/her deepest thoughts, which he/she may not be able to articulate. It does mean that we give the child ample opportunities to speak from the heart in any way that is comfortable. This may involve music, or drawing, or crafts, or playing with dolls, etc. It is this type of environment that enables the child to speak his/her feelings to the adult, without necessarily using words.

In telling a child that someone he/she loves has died, try to do so quickly in familiar surroundings by someone whom the child trusts. Avoid jargon. Be natural and loving, answering questions truthfully in an age-appropriate vocabulary. Avoid the abstract and theoretical, remembering that we should not link suffering and death with sin and divine punishment. Parents with strong religious convictions can share these convictions, provided they are sincere. If, for example, you do not believe in life after death, do not speak about it. In short, avoid lying, for children sense when an adult is lying to them. Remember that children often blame themselves for the death of a family member, so the adult needs to be sensitive to defuse that mistaken notion.

> He couldn't stop crying. I held my son tightly, trying to comfort him, but not knowing what was wrong. It was as if a nightmare had crashed through his waking hours, forcing him to confront in the light what he feared in the dark. I sensed his sobs had something to do with my father who had died several months before. However, I,

too, was grieving, and was not sure how to handle my
own feelings of abandonment and loss. The truth came
out at breakfast the next morning when he apologized to
me for causing such pain. "I didn't want Poppy to die,"
he cried. "I didn't know he would get sick when we were
playing in the snow."

Do not be alarmed when some activities appear
inappropriate; for example, a child, upon hearing of his/
her father's death, goes out to play stickball with his
friends while the family remains in the house weeping.
This could indicate that the loss is too difficult to process
at the time, and the child needs to do so on his/her own
terms.

Be careful about covering up the event with fiction.
For example, telling a child that mommy went to heaven
because God thought mommy was so good Jesus wanted
her to be with the angels, will not help the child deal with
the reality of death. Such an approach can cause irreparable damage that prevents the child from grieving in a
healthy fashion. It is precisely at this time that a child
needs to rely upon an adult's giving him/her information
that is truthful. For example, saying that daddy went on a
long journey might bring about the fear of abandonment
within the child as he/she struggles with the pain of
feeling deserted in that daddy did not say good-bye.
Comparing death to sleep can also be frightening to a
small child who now fears closing his/her eyes at night.
Equating sickness with death can also lead a child to
assume that a cold or cough will cause death. In short, we
need to be careful and sensitive in the way we communicate to children that someone they love has died.

PRAYING THROUGH GRIEF

A wonderful resource for learning how to pray
through grief is the book *Healing the Greatest Hurt*
(Mahwah, NJ: Paulist Press, 1984), by Matthew Linn,
Dennis Linn, and Sheila Fabricant. They remind us that
prayer does more than help us let go of our beloved.
Prayer teaches us how Jesus will be with us and our
beloved now that our loved one is with the Lord.
Through prayer we realize that we can be closer than
ever before to the deceased, as love and forgiveness
continue to flow through Jesus to us, and back through
Jesus to the one we have offered back to God (2 Corinthians 5:17-21 / 1 Peter 4:6).

PSYCHICS, MEDIUMS, SÉANCES, AND ANCESTOR WORSHIP

Praying through grief, however, is not to be confused
with ancestor worship, or with the practice of contacting
the dead through séances, or striving to consult the dead
through others, for example, a Christian psychic (which,
really, is a contradictory term). These means are ex-
pressly forbidden by God's word and by the teaching of
the Church. *Healing the Greatest Hurt* clearly explains
the difference between prayer for the deceased and the
use of mediums or psychics to contact the dead. First,
there is no use of a medium but only prayer to Jesus
Christ. Thus there is no giving up of one's identity to be
controlled by another, but rather a conscious free relationship with Jesus. Second, there is no person calling up
the spirits to be physically present, but rather we focus on

Jesus first and then ask him to gather our departed loved
ones however he chooses. Third, there is no replacing of
the guidance of God by the guidance of the deceased, but
only asking that the deceased be intercessors leading us
deeper into God's guidance. There is no intimating that
the deceased are more powerful or loving than God, but
only reverence for the deceased as members of Jesus'
body who can channel his infinite power and love.

For the Christian, therefore, the question is not
whether a psychic or medium *can* contact the dead, but
whether one *should* contact the dead. Here the Church
and the Scriptures give very clear directions: *No*. There
are several pastoral reasons why we are told not to be
involved with anyone who contacts the dead. First, we
can be fooled by a false spirit. Second, we can be tricked
by fraud. Third, we can be manipulated by an unscrupulous person taking advantage of one who is grieving. This
can cause long-term, adverse effects, in that the natural
and important process of letting go of our deceased loved
ones is curtailed by our attempts to continually recontact
relatives or friends who have died. In addition, a grieving
family can grow overly dependent upon the psychic or
medium, thus setting up an unhealthy relationship that
can consciously or unconsciously manipulate those who
are grieving.

Remember, the question is not whether or not we can
contact the dead. The question is the way we contact the
dead. Our faith tells us that the only "medium" we are to
have is Jesus Christ in the power of God's Holy Spirit. In
Jesus we are made new; in Jesus alone we live forever.
As we remain close to Jesus the Lord, we are, in a certain

sense, "communing" with those who have died. There is
no other way if we intend to experience true wholeness
through the grieving process.

THREE SIMPLE STEPS

I know of no better way to pray through grief than to
follow the three simple steps listed in *Healing the
Greatest Hurt*. First, we share our heart with Jesus,
telling him how we are feeling, not worrying about
whether our feelings involve anger or negative thoughts.
We simply relate to Jesus where we're at during this time
of pain, in our grief, through the tears. It helps when we
ask Jesus to grieve with us. During our time of prayer,
therefore, picture Jesus weeping with us over the loss of
our loved one.

In the second step, we ask Jesus to reconcile us with
our loved one. This is sometimes difficult as we allow
Jesus to bring to our mind and heart situations where we
wish we had acted differently toward the deceased.
During a lifetime of loving, there is also a lifetime of
mistakes made, words spoken, gestures misunderstood,
etc. As we pray through grief, we are given the opportunity to be reconciled for those times, whether they
represent a major or minor breakdown of loving. During
this type of prayer, we tell Jesus and our beloved what we
wish had happened or what we wish we had said. We
then picture Jesus holding both of us, and speaking his
healing words of love. During this prayer it is important
to keep in mind that our loved one, now loving with
Jesus' love because he/she is united to the Lord, is more
than able and willing to forgive us and accept our

forgiveness. In fact, it is guaranteed. Prayer of this type, done over a period of time, enables Jesus to free us from any unhealed relationship between ourselves and the deceased, as well as between the deceased and others.

The third step in this type of prayer is to give thanks to God not only for the new life that our loved one now experiences in the Lord, but also for the new life that continues to come to us through our relationship with the deceased. Praying this way enables us to thank God for the gifts we received in our relationship with our loved one. Undoubtedly they are gifts that helped us to grow, even when pain was involved—for example, the gift of learning how to forgive, the gift of discovering more about our own strengths and weaknesses, or the gift of being stretched to reach out to others now that we are alone. Back at step one, these may not have appeared to be gifts at all, rather difficulties that had to be overcome. Now, however, confident that Jesus enables us to continue relating to our loved one in a new and vibrant way, we are able to celebrate all the ways that this new relationship will help us grow in love with God and with others.

QUESTIONS ABOUT PURGATORY

Sometimes a grieving person is unable to pray through grief because he/she is overwhelmed with doubt about how the Lord has embraced the person who has died. All too often, we take upon ourselves the role of judge and jury rather than allowing the God who is mercy and love to do and accomplish what God does best: namely, to bring into the fullness of life all those whom he has created. We need to remember, therefore, that heaven and hell are not ours to give away. The Lord alone is the one who determines how a person is to spend eternity. Our limited notions of God's eternal plan of salvation can cause us undue anxiety and pain as we speculate how God is going to treat someone who, perhaps, has not "followed the rules." We tend to forget that, although the Church teaches that hell exists, the Church has never stated that someone has been condemned to hell forever. In addition, we tend to forget that purgatory is not a place of punishment, but rather a time of healing, where the deceased who have failed to love in this life (and who among us will not be included in this category?) are given the opportunity to be healed by God so that they can love throughout eternity. Thinking back to Chapter One, which describes the goal of the Christian life as self-giving, the pain often associated with purgatory might be described as the pain that occurs as God helps us surrender our self-centeredness so that we can allow God's selfless love to grow within us.

Our prayer for the souls in purgatory, therefore, is not so much a prayer begging God to allow the deceased entry into the kingdom, as much as praying that they will be open to the fullness of love that God wishes to give them—a love that allows them to live forever in the light of Jesus. This understanding of purgatory and God's healing love can give new meaning to the phrase *born again* when applied to the Christian life.

Prayer for those in purgatory, therefore, is an important part of the healing process not just for the deceased, but also for those who mourn. As part of our own healing during this time of pain and doubt, remember to pray for those who have died.

CONCLUSION

Throughout the grieving process, be aware that pride can do a great deal of damage. Perhaps this takes you by surprise, in that pride is not usually associated with grieving. Unfortunately, our current cultural milieu accentuates a rugged individualism that is quite contrary to the movement of God's grace in the world and in our lives. Many of us, because of upbringing and training, are too proud to seek or accept help. When asked how we are feeling, we automatically respond with a word that blocks entry into our heart; we say *fine*, when in reality we are coming apart at the seams. Thinking that we can do it ourselves, we fail to recognize how unprepared we are when death comes to someone we love.

Pride, therefore, can easily become a barrier to healing as we overcompensate for our hurt by ignoring it during those times when family and friends have been sent by God to bring the Lord's healing presence.

CHAPTER FIVE

FREQUENTLY ASKED QUESTIONS

Q. My spouse was a veteran, but the priest would not let the flag remain on my husband's coffin when it entered the church. Why not?

A.   The pall, symbolizing our baptism with Christ and our Christian dignity as God's children, is the traditional covering for a casket as it enters the church for the funeral liturgy. For that reason the flag is removed when the coffin is brought into the church, and the pall is placed on the coffin when the celebrant greets the body at the door of the church.

Q. If a person is not anointed before dying, will he/she go to heaven?

A.   The sacrament of anointing is the Church's sacrament of healing. It is not a person's passport to heaven. Previous to Vatican II, anointing a person was called Extreme Unction, and was usually seen as indicating a person's imminent death. The Church teaches that a person's faith in Jesus Christ and his/her participation in the life of the community of believers are what prepares a person for entrance into the kingdom of heaven.

Q. How long should the wake be?

A. Much depends upon custom and your own need. It's important that the length of time for the wake be suitable so that the grieving process is not curtailed. Some families find that two nights are adequate, giving them time to contact friends and family without putting additional stress upon the family itself. (Should additional time be needed for arranging travel and/or contacting family, most funeral homes will delay the wake at no additional charge.) Some families (and faiths) have a one-day viewing followed by the burial. The grieving process then continues in the home as family and friends offer comfort and companionship to the family. In short, there is no pat answer. Do what is comfortable, remembering that long wake periods can put undue strain upon the family.

Q. Since the deceased never went to mass, couldn't we just have the priest come to the funeral home?

A. For the believer, participating in the funeral liturgies is an important part of the grieving process in that it helps us remember where our hope lies: namely, in Jesus' own death and resurrection. The purpose of these rites, therefore, is not for the deceased as much as for those who mourn. We who remain need to surround ourselves with the symbols of our faith so we can make sense of that which the world claims is senseless.

Q. I'd like to donate a memorial to the parish in memory of the deceased. What should I do?

A. Avoid purchasing items for the church without first discovering what items the church needs. All too often a parish receives vestments, cruets, lectionaries, etc., and has little use for them. Unfortunately, liturgical items can be expensive, far exceeding a family's means. For that reason, some parishes set up memorial guilds to pool memorial offerings so that important items can be purchased as needed.

Q. Can we be cremated?
A. The Church allows cremation provided it is not chosen as a way of denying Christian teaching, especially that of the resurrection of the dead and the immortality of the soul. Although permitted, it does not enjoy the same value as burial of the body, which is preferred. The reason for this preference is the long-standing practice of burying the body of the deceased in a grave or tomb in imitation of the burial of Jesus' body.

Q. Can the cremated remains be present at the funeral liturgy?
A. The Church strongly prefers that the body of the deceased be present for the funeral rites since the pres-ence of the body most clearly brings to mind the life and death of the person. For this reason, when cremation is chosen, it is recommended that it take place after the funeral liturgy. There are times, however, when this may not be possible—for example, when the cremated remains are taken to another location for burial. In such cases, the cremated remains can be present for the full course of the funeral rites. The funeral mass, of course, should be celebrated in the church.

Q. I want to leave my body to science. Does that mean I can't have a funeral mass?

A. When a person wills his/her body to science, it is impossible for the body to be present at the funeral liturgy. This does not mean that a person is deprived of the Church's burial rites. It simply means that the body cannot be present during that time.

Q. In my parish, the priest did not say the rosary at the wake service. Is that what happens in other parishes?

A. Depending upon local custom, a rosary or decade of the rosary is often prayed at some time during the time of the wake. The official vigil prayers for the deceased, however, involve readings from Scripture, time for reflection, intercessions, and other prayers that do not include the rosary. This is because the rosary is a personal and private devotion, whereas the funeral rites are public, liturgical prayers said by the Church for its members. The proclamation of God's word from the Scripture is very important during the mourning period because it keeps us focused on our hope in Jesus' victory over death.

Q. In my parish, some lay people came and offered the prayers at the wake service. Why didn't the priest come?

A. More and more parishes have come to realize that the privilege of burying the dead belongs to the entire people of God, not to the priest alone. Each member of the Body of Christ has a particular role to play. For that reason, parishes are empowering teams of lay people to participate in this process by attending the wake and leading the community in prayer and reflection; attending the funeral

mass as a way of supporting those who are mourning;
and providing some type of aftercare service, such as
bereavement groups, to help families cope in the months
that follow the actual burial. The priest's role in this
process is to preside at the celebration of the Eucharist, a
role that only he can fulfill. The other roles, however, can
be done by other members of the community, thus
helping more people perform the corporal works of
mercy, one of which is burying the dead.

Q. Must I be buried in a Catholic cemetery?
A.   Although the Church has moved away from a
legislative stance that mandated burial in a Catholic
cemetery, it is important to emphasize that the Catholic
cemetery remains the usual and proper place for the
burial of Catholics in view of the values contained in the
Church's burial tradition. It is in a Catholic cemetery that
our faith is reaffirmed through the signs and symbols
used throughout the cemetery grounds, the care and
reverence shown the human body as the temple of the
Spirit, as well as the witness of faith in the resurrection
and support offered by the Church community. This
union with Christ and the community was evident in the
early catacombs, which served not only as burial places,
but also as places for the celebration of the Eucharist.
Catholic cemeteries, therefore, speak the special message
of Christian belief in the abundance of eternal life to a
world that, at times, seeks the fullness of life within the
passing realities of space and time. Catholic cemeteries
proclaim the sublime mysteries of faith in a personal
God, of hope in the resurrection, and of the glorious
reunion of the members of Christ's Mystical Body.

Q. If the deceased liked a particular song, can I request that song for the funeral mass?

A. During the funeral mass, it is important that the hymns we sing focus our attention on the saving mystery of Jesus. Remember that it is through Jesus' death and resurrection that our hope of resurrection dawns. Favorite songs, especially secular songs, therefore, are usually inappropriate for inclusion in the funeral rites. Favorite hymns, however, may be used if the lyrics direct our attention to the death and resurrection of Jesus.

Q. Is it worthwhile purchasing a burial plot ahead of time?

A. Purchasing a burial plot ahead of time gives you the opportunity to pay for the plot over a period of time. It also removes the burden of having your family make an emotion-laden decision during a time of stress and grief. In addition, a plot purchased at the time of death must be paid for in full before interment, thereby putting additional pressure on the family.

Q. How much should it cost for the funeral home?

A. Depending upon geographic location and services provided, the cost of a funeral can vary substantially. It is not unreasonable, however, to pay from $2,500 to $3,500 for a traditional funeral. (The national average is approximately $3,350.) This includes a metal casket as well as the usual services of a funeral director, excluding cemetery or religious service fees.

In making arrangements, be careful that you are not swayed by false or disparaging statements made by directors who try to sell higher-priced hardwood caskets by making critical remarks about the cloth-covered or metal casket you may have chosen (e.g., "If that's your personal choice, then we'll simply go with it"). The fact is, one does not have to purchase a hardwood casket to provide a reverent and honorable means of burial. Keep in mind that Christians are expected to show honor to the deceased's body, which was a temple of the Holy Spirit, but that does not imply that we are to preserve the body for any length of time. For this reason, purchasing caskets which supposedly offer protective seals, lawn crypts, or mausoleums, though available in Catholic cemeteries, are quite out of order in light of our Christian belief in the resurrection of the body.

In that there are so many financial variables in arranging for a funeral, it is helpful to make arrangements before they are needed. Therefore, do not hesitate to visit the funeral homes in your area and discuss costs with the funeral directors. Prices can even be acquired over the phone, since the FTC requires all mortuaries to provide this information. In doing this, you will be able to know ahead of time what to expect. It will also allow you to make decisions such as casket type, number of days, etc.—all of which influence the cost—without the stress and sense of urgency that surrounds us when we actually need these services.

Medicaid applicants or recipients might consider prepayment by arranging an irrevocable trust with the funeral home. *Such a fund must be used for burial arrangements only*, though they can be transferred to another funeral home should you wish. Proceeding in this direction removes the worry of having adequate funds for burial arrangements should medical or nursing home costs deplete a person's savings. When proceeding in this direction, however, be aware that some consumer groups do not recommend paying for the funeral home in advance. Although it is helpful to prearrange for the funeral, avoid signing a prepayment plan unless you have the contract checked by a lawyer.

Q. What should I look for in choosing a funeral director?

A. Look for someone who has compassion, and is willing to work with you, rather than force his/her own opinions upon you. Although most funeral directors are people of integrity who see their work as a service for the community, it is still very easy for a director to convince a person to choose a style of funeral that is beyond what is necessary and beyond the person's financial capabilities.

Q. What can I expect the funeral director to do?

A. Depending upon local custom, a funeral director will: prepare the body for viewing; help you choose the type of wake service that will meet your family's needs—for example, the amount of time allotted for the wake, the size of the room, flowers and mementos that might be displayed—and take care of publishing the obituary. In addition, funeral directors will make the arrangements with the cemetery and the church. They often provide memorial cards that can be distributed to those who come to offer their condolences. Many funeral parlors offer additional services that help families cope with grieving.

This may take the form of workshops throughout the year, as well as literature that can help families better understand the grieving process.

Q.   How much does the church charge for a funeral mass?
A.   There is no set fee for a funeral mass. Most churches request a donation to cover the cost of music as well as the services provided by the parish. These services necessarily include year-round maintenance, which allows the church and the staff to be there when you need them. Funeral donations, therefore, are used to cover those costs. They are not a rental fee for using the church during the actual time of the funeral mass. Most parishes will make arrangements for families that cannot make the suggested donation.

Q.   I haven't been to church in a long time. I want very much to receive holy communion at my spouse's funeral. Am I allowed?
A.   In such situations it is helpful to contact the rectory and make arrangements to speak with a priest. He will help you through this difficult time so you can experience the healing power of God's love in the sacrament of reconciliation. A great deal has changed in the Church's understanding of this sacrament and the way it is cel- ebrated. More than likely, you will find it a powerful time of grace that will strengthen you in the days following the funeral mass.

Q.   I want to choose the readings at the funeral mass. Am I allowed to choose two readings from the New

Testament rather than an Old Testament and New Testament reading?

A.   We are given the option of choosing two readings before the priest or deacon reads the Gospel at the funeral mass. If this option is taken, an Old Testament reading and a New Testament reading with a sung Responsorial Psalm in between are the usual choices. For pastoral reasons, however, a family may substitute a New Testament reading for the Old Testament reading.

Q.   I want to read a poem at the funeral mass, but the priest would not allow it. Why not?

A.   The funeral mass is meant to celebrate the reality of Christ's death and resurrection in our midst. For that purpose, we use the sacred writings of our faith, the Scriptures, to remind ourselves that our hope lies in Jesus. For that reason, reading a favorite poem or prose selection is more appropriate at the Vigil for the Deceased (the wake service).

Q.   I wanted to give a eulogy at the funeral mass, but was told it can't be done. I've been to parishes where there were eulogies. How come my parish does not allow it?

A.   The best time to offer a eulogy is at the Vigil for the Deceased, that is, at the wake service. At that time, we can remember the ways the deceased has helped us experience love, and allow other members of our family and friends to share their reflections. The funeral mass, however, is meant to focus on the paschal mystery celebrated in the breaking of the bread, which offers us hope in the resurrection of the body. Eulogies, therefore, are best done at the Vigil.

Q. I went to a funeral mass in another parish. They had a lay woman walking next to the priest during the entrance procession. Is that allowed?
A.   Many parishes have begun to invite parishioners to assist in burying the dead. Teams of lay people, therefore, are available to lector at the funeral mass, help with the distribution of communion, provide a type of "honor guard" for the casket as the pallbearers bring the body into the church, and assist with other responsibilities. Undoubtedly, you have experienced one or more members of such a team working with the priest as the parish fulfills the Church's exhortation to bury the dead, which is one of the corporal works of mercy that all of God's people are called to embrace.

Q.   What is an aftercare program? My parish priest told me that it would help me a lot.
A.   An aftercare program helps those who mourn cope with the death of a loved one. It often begins several weeks or months after the actual burial. It can involve several dimensions, depending upon the parish's resources: phone calls, visits to the home, notes and letters of encouragement during difficult holiday periods, bereavement groups, special liturgies of remembrance, etc.

Q.   How long should I wait before joining a bereavement group?

A. Each person has different needs. A basic rule of thumb, however, is to allow several months to pass before joining a bereavement group.

Q. Is it necessary to put a death notice or obituary in the newspaper?

A. Although not necessary, death notices help communicate specific information that people need to know if they wish to express their condolences: for example, the times of the wake, the location and time of the funeral mass, etc.

Q. I was told that people often get robbed while they are at the wake or funeral mass. Is this true?

A. It's hard to get reliable statistics in this area. One must be cautious, however, since there are unscrupulous people who take advantage of those who are grieving. Families, therefore, need to make sure that homes remain well-lit during the times they are attending the wake, and, if possible, that the homes be occupied. Friends and neighbors can be helpful in providing this service.

Q. My friend is a deacon. Is he able to preach at the funeral mass if I ask him?

A. Most deacons have permission to preach on such occasions. As a matter of courtesy, make sure that the parish priest is informed if this is your desire. The funeral director will help you make such arrangements.

Q. Should I take my children to the wake or funeral mass? They appear so young, I'm afraid they will be wounded for life by the experience.

A.   When helping children grieve, it is important that we do not deny them the opportunity to express their feelings or experience the visual realization of death. Denying these realities does not make them go away. Thinking that a child will be wounded for life may really be a projection of our own discomfort with wakes and funerals. Be aware, therefore, of that possibility. Don't be afraid of tears, for example. Deal with the situation honestly and simply without using fairy-tale jargon. This builds trust, and shows that the subject can be broached again at a later time, as the child becomes aware of additional questions and concerns. In offering your response, avoid answering your own questions when answering the child's questions. It is easy to communicate your own anxiety to the child.

Consider using some visual aids to help the child experience the reality of death in a loving environment. For example, displaying memorabilia or special gifts that the child associates with the deceased offers a tangible sign that links the memory of a life lived and shared with the natural reality of death.

When dealing with teenagers, be conscious that their philosophy of life often is not big enough to handle death, in that their life experience is still limited. Sometimes teens require additional counseling to help them through the grieving time.

Remember to include the children as much as possible, without forcing them to do what they express as uncomfortable. A rule of thumb is that if they are old enough to go to church, they probably are old enough to go to the funeral.

As believers, try to communicate to children that death is part of the life process in which all partake. Although changes occur because of death, our life remains supported by a faith that the human spirit cannot be overcome by physical forces. In taking this approach, death reveals to us the depth of life—life here and the life that is yet to come.

APPENDIX A

A FUNERAL CHECKLIST

It will be helpful to bring the following information and items of the deceased when making arrangements with the funeral director:

IMPORTANT ITEMS

- Date of Birth
- Place of Birth (City and State, or Country)
- Father's Name
- Mother's Maiden Name
- Social Security Number
- Highest Education Level
- Occupation (Employer and Address)
- Discharge Papers if Veteran
- Cemetery Deed
- Recent Photograph
- Full Set of Clothing (including undergarments)
- Jewelry
- Cosmetics

TO-DO LIST

- Working with the funeral home, determine an appropriate length of time for the wake, the place of the funeral mass, and the cemetery.

- Contact family, close friends, and employer. This can be done by phone. It's helpful to have a list made and ask others to assist you in this area.

- Choose a small selection of flowers for the wake. A reputable florist will help you here. Do not go overboard. The money for flowers, which last a very brief time, is better spent as a memorial donation to a worthy charity.

- If an obituary is needed, give the funeral director the necessary facts. Funeral directors usually take care of notifying the newspapers.

- Insurance companies need to be notified, as well as a lawyer and the executor of the person's will. Death certificates will be needed for banking and insurance purposes.

- Arrange for child care as well as meals for the next few days. Do not hesitate to accept the help of neighbors in this area. Most want to help and will do a fine job of relieving you of the burden.

- You will need to notify distant friends and relatives. Sometimes a printed note sent to all with a brief handwritten sentence or two on the bottom of the

note will suffice, depending on your own
personality and your closeness to those who live far
away.

- Arrange to send acknowledgment cards to all who
  send flowers, money, gifts, etc. Printed acknowledg-
  ments that have space for handwritten notes are
  appropriate.

- Check promptly on all credit card and debt install-
  ments. The insurance company may cover these
  debts. If there is a delay in meeting payments,
  contact the companies involved lest penalties
  accumulate.

- Carefully check all life and casualty insurance, and
  death benefits, including social security, credit
  unions, trade unions, etc. It is possible that survivors
  are entitled to income from these sources.

- If the deceased is living alone, contact the utility
  company, landlord, post office, etc.

ADDENDUM

Many people keep important papers in a bank's
safety deposit box as a way of preserving family records.
Since these records are often needed when arranging for
a burial, it is a good idea to keep copies in your home
files so you might reference them when needed. This will
avoid unnecessary delays should the bank be closed
when you need the papers to arrange for a burial.

APPENDIX B

EXPERIENCES OF GRIEF

We know that grieving is a process, one involving various stages through which all of us pass at some time or another. In order to expand upon the five stages mentioned in Chapter Four (denial, anger, bargaining, despair, acceptance), the following chart and explanation are offered to help identify the smaller steps we take during the five major stages cited by Dr. Elisabeth Kübler-Ross. These smaller steps along with the diagram come from notes taken during a bereavement course sponsored by the Archdiocese of New York, taught by the late Demon Dewey.

As you can see from the diagram, there is a great deal of movement throughout the process. We move back and forth, and up and down. Internally we probably feel as if we are going nowhere fast, when, in reality, each step we take is an important part of the journey. Do not be dismayed, therefore, if you appear to be moving one step ahead and then two steps backwards. It's all part of the journey to wholeness.

Experiences of Grief

Disbelief, Shock

Sobbing/Crying

Physical Symptoms

Why?

Denial

Repetition

Confusion

Reality of Death

Idealization

Anxiety/Panic

Relief/Laughter

Bargaining

Depression

Expectations

Preoccupation

Lowered Self-Esteem

Guilt

Anger · · Loneliness

Despair

Life Is Worth Living

New Life Patterns

Missing

Hope Emerges

Limbo

Bitterness

Envy

Hatred

Frustration

Sadness

Helplessness

DISBELIEF

"It can't be true." You keep thinking that in any minute you will awake from the bad dream or nightmare that has been consuming your psychic energy. Sometimes you cannot even cry because you don't really believe it happened. People will comment on how well you are doing, but you know that you appear to be doing so well because you just don't believe it.

SHOCK

Shock is nature's way of softening the blow. It serves as a cushion—giving us time to absorb the fact of loss. One hears the words, but does not understand the full impact. Emotions seem frozen. Disorientation, restless-ness, numbness, bewilderment, and inability to think overcome us. It takes everything just to function. Our motions become robot-like; we feel as if we were an observer, watching this terrible tragedy happen to someone else. Later, people tell of the kindness of friends.

SOBBING/CRYING

Sobbing means to weep aloud with short, gasping breaths. It is an important outlet for the deep, strong emotions that accompany the death of a loved one. Some people cry often and frequently, while others push their tears deep inside. One thing is certain: it is helpful to cry—to release all that pent-up emotion. Whether we cry alone or with others, take the time to cry. Those who advise us to "control ourselves" or "be strong for the kids" are offering very poor counsel. Accept the grief. Do not feign bravery by holding back the tears. At first, one needs to take time to grieve daily. Looking at pictures and mementos, or playing special music, may aid in releasing our tears. This advice applies to both women and men, for both need the healing power of tears to calm their inner spirit. Crying is a good model for children. When adults cry, children learn to share their feelings, instead of pushing them down and struggling alone.

PHYSICAL SYMPTOMS

One may experience some of the following:

- Lack or increase of appetite
- Sleeplessness or oversleeping
- A knot or emptiness in the pit of our stomach
- Tightness in the throat
- Shaky legs
- Headaches
- Stomach cramps
- Sighing to catch your breath
- Trembling, chills, fatigue
- Chest pains, general discomfort
- Difficulty swallowing and/or speaking
- Digestive disorders (nausea, diarrhea, indigestion)
- Feeling weak or faint
- Temporary paralysis in limbs
- Temporary loss of sight

Some of these symptoms may be part of the grieving process. Should they arise and remain for an inordinate amount of time, see a medical doctor. Take care of yourself by establishing a simple routine. Exercise and sleep will often help lift the depression.

DENIAL

It takes time to believe that someone we love has died. It is not unusual, therefore, to act as if our loved one were still alive: inadvertently setting a place at the table, buying his/her favorite food, speaking with a friend and commenting, "I have to tell my wife/husband about this." Do not be alarmed when you mistake another person for the deceased, especially when walking through a store or on a crowded street. In the beginning stages of grief, it is normal and should not be feared.

WHY?

Often we keep asking, "Why?" Why did he/she have to die? We do not expect an answer, but we ask the question repeatedly in an effort to make sense of the loss. Although the question remains unanswered, it is important to keep asking the question until we can take the step of letting the question go.

REPETITION

You find that you keep repeating the same words, the same stories, the same feelings to those around you. Having a friend who simply listens, especially one who has experienced a similar loss, can be helpful at this time.

Don't be concerned that you keep repeating yourself. Just be yourself, tears and all.

REALITY OF DEATH

This is a frightening time in the grieving process. We feel we have been getting worse, not better. Often this happens after people who have helped us by their presence begin to leave you alone and return to their normal routines. The fact of the person's death stares at you through the void. The best advice is to lean into the pain. As much as we do not want to experience the hurt, we must in order for healing to take place.

CONFUSION

The simplest decisions now seem impossible. Your ability to concentrate evaporates regardless of how hard you try to focus on a topic. Disorganization and errors frame the areas of your life which were once under control. You feel impatient, wanting to do something, but remain unclear as to what to do. What's worse is the feeling that you simply don't have the energy to do anything in the first place! Weariness appears to have won out.

ANXIETY/PANIC (FEAR OF LOSING CONTROL)

It creeps up on us. At first we may fear being alone during the night; then during parts of the day. We worry about the future, and fear that something will happen to other members of our family. Special dates, such as birthdays and holidays, cause additional anxiety, especially the days immediately preceding the event. We wonder how we'll get through them. The smallest concern now appears larger than we can handle. The slightest "unknown" throws us off kilter, causing us to think that we're going crazy. Sometimes bereaved people harbor thoughts of suicide, thinking this is their only way to escape the physical and emotional pain. We panic at the prospect of always feeling this way.

The situation may seem hopeless, but panic is normal. If it becomes intolerable, however, we need to talk to someone about these feelings.

IDEALIZATION

During this time, we highlight the deceased's best qualities, often to the point of exaggeration. Suddenly he/she becomes "perfect" in every respect: the best parents, the most talented child, the most loving spouse, etc. Though such praise does not harm anyone, we need to remain sensitive to others in the family, especially siblings, who may feel put down when compared to your praise-filled description of the deceased.

BARGAINING

We want things back the way they were, or at least we want some sign that the dead are resting peacefully. We often make promises to ourselves and to God during this time, hoping that the fulfillment of these promises will forestall other tragedies taking place in our life.

DEPRESSION

You hurt so much you become immobilized. Mornings are terrible. Simply getting out of bed or preparing a small meal becomes a large effort. Nothing matters anymore. You give up caring for yourself physically, often appearing disheveled when people visit. Talking to others during this time is a concrete action that may help lessen the feelings of depression.

If our depression becomes severe, professional help is advisable. Signs of severe depression may be: loss of appetite, insomnia, inability to enjoy anything, anxiety, apathy, preoccupation with thoughts of suicide, wishing you were dead, loss of interest in sex, lack of concentration, inability to make decisions, loss of memory, irritability, feelings of worthlessness, inability to cry even when you want to, intense guilt, and withdrawal from family and friends. Note that all those who grieve experience some of these symptoms at various times. If six or more of these symptoms become severe and continue over an extended period of time, however, professional help may be required.

RELIEF (LAUGHTER)

This phase comes and goes. Often after a particularly troublesome time, you feel better and may even think that the worst is over. There is a temporary sense of relief at no longer feeling down. You begin to look forward to enjoying yourself. Take advantage of these times. Try to nurture a sense of humor, which bereaved people report as being helpful in the healing process. Feelings of disloyalty or betrayal may arise at this time when you realize that you've started to enjoy something again. These feelings, however, are not meant to measure or judge your relationship with the deceased.

EXPECTATIONS

More often than not, we place unrealistic expectations upon ourselves. We want to handle the grief better than we think we are doing; we want to "get over it" faster than is humanly possible. Added to this are the unrealistic expectations of others: "You should be over your grief by now." We think we will feel better as soon as the holidays are over, or as soon as the anniversary passes, etc. Such expectations only hinder the grief process. It is far better to throw away our timetables of how we think we should feel by such and such a date. Taking one day at a time, or one half-day at a time, or one hour at a time, is far more realistic.

LOWERED SELF-ESTEEM

An average person's self-esteem usually rates around seventy out of one hundred. Generally speaking, however, a bereaved person's self-esteem is in the teens! In other words, it happens to everyone who grieves, so do not be concerned.

PREOCCUPATION

You think of nothing but your loss. Your dreams, your waking moments, and your conversations all focus on the deceased. Usually this lessens with time.

GUILT

Many are tortured with the "if only," the "what if," and the "should have." "If only I had called sooner";

"What if I hadn't stopped for cigarettes?"; "I should have known better than to give him the car." In short, we tend to blame ourselves for things we think we did, or didn't do, or wish we had done, that appear to be associated with our loved one's death. Such feelings, though normal, are unrealistic. Try not to submerge the guilt where you can no longer identify it or speak about it to others. Hopefully time will help us realize that we did the best we could under the circumstances. This is especially true when dealing with suicide, where it is important to remember that we cannot control the behavior of another person.

ANGER

Anger may be directed at ourselves, family members, spouses, medical personnel, God, those who caused the accident, and so on. In addition, it is not unusual to direct our anger toward those who we believe are rushing us in the grieving process or those who try to pretend that nothing ever happened.

Although anger is normal, suppressing anger can cause serious physical difficulties, and lead us deeper into depression. It is important, therefore, to find ways to express our anger, even though our attempts to do so might appear odd—for example, screaming aloud in the privacy of our room, hitting a pillow, etc. Talking with someone about our anger will help us define, understand, and deal with the anger in a healthy way.

LONELINESS

After the initial outpouring of condolences, personal assistance, premade meals, sympathy cards, and calls, our support system often fades away as friends, coworkers, and neighbors resume their daily routines. We soon become isolated in our grief. Often the very people who comforted us during the wake and funeral find it difficult to relate to us now that the burial is over. They avoid us or continually change the subject because they do not know how to act or speak about death.

In reality, few people are able to understand the pain that emerges during this time, unless, of course, they themselves have made the journey already. For this reason, bereavement groups are a helpful resource for those who find themselves feeling lonely due to the absence of the deceased.

DESPAIR

You may come to the point where the agony seems intolerable. You think that you simply cannot survive any longer. Your hopes and dreams, dashed now by death's power, strangle your reasons for continuing. Feelings of desperation, despondency, pessimism, and loss of all hope surround you. Although it appears darker than ever before, be assured at this point that it is always darkest before the burden of grief begins to lift. Speaking with someone who has gone through this experience can be very comforting.

SADNESS

Deprived of our loved one's presence, we feel unhappy, inconsolable, distressed, sorrowful, dejected, and heartbroken.

HELPLESSNESS

The thought, "What am I going to do?" fills every waking moment. We feel helpless about our feelings, our situation, our grief, our life. We feel unable to cope or improve. Self-pity often invades during this time. Although we know intellectually that we had no control over the death of our loved one, we feel a sense of powerlessness at not having been able to prevent it.

ENVY

You may feel jealous of people who still have their loved ones to enjoy. With a child's death, dreams of his/her future are gone—college, jobs, weddings, grandchildren—things you would have shared together.

FRUSTRATION

We become upset with ourselves, disappointed that we are not coping as well as we think we should. Many impulses, thoughts, feelings, and actions that had become habitual are stopped in midcourse. We are left with these unfulfilled emotions, desires, and thoughts buzzing about in our head, or creating a knot in our stomach.

RESENTMENT/BITTERNESS/HATRED

Bereaved people often feel resentful about the death and their changed circumstances. Sometimes there is an unconscious hostility towards others whose families are still intact. Some bereaved people feel hatred toward those responsible for the death. These bitter feelings need to be recognized and worked on, or the bitterness could last for many years. Hatred and bitterness drain you of energy, destroying your health and relationships with others. When these feelings are ignored, healing is blocked.

LIMBO

Eventually we may reach an important doorway between the reality of death and the point where life seems worthwhile again. We may feel a little better at last, but uncertain of what to do next. It may take much longer than we would like before our zest for living returns. We often live behind a facade, masking our feelings by telling everyone, "I'm fine."

HOPE EMERGES

You realize that your grief is softening. At first the pain was with you constantly. Now the pain of grief is briefer, coming less frequently. The good days outnumber the bad. You feel encouraged, and begin to believe that you will get better. Activities that previously had been so painful—housework, future events, etc.—become part of your life again. Once again, you are effective at work and at home. You are now able to make decisions and handle problems; you are able to sleep and eat as you had in the past. You finally begin to care again about others. Life starts moving forward: you smile and laugh once again, and are rewarded with the smiles of family and friends.

MISSING

You will always miss your loved one. Special family events—such as holidays, birthdays, anniversaries—or even a song or special TV program will trigger the feelings of longing and loss. Seeing other families enjoy a special event also deepens your feelings of yearning. You cannot help but wish your loved one were alive. You miss countless things that were special about your relationship—a hug, a kiss, a smile, a phone call, or hearing the words, "I love you."

STRUGGLE WITH NEW LIFE PATTERNS

You realize that you have a choice: you *can* rebuild a new life. It will be different without your loved one, but life can be enjoyed again. It is important to seek meaning in living. Learn how to make happiness happen in your life.

If you are grieving the death of a child, work hard at restoring the marriage bond between you and your spouse. Statistics show that more than 70 percent of such marriages end in separation or divorce unless the couples consciously work at maintaining their marriage. In short, one needs to reinvest oneself in marriage, work, activities, and friends. New friends can be found among others who are going through a similar process. You may find it necessary or helpful to move, find a job, or do volunteer work. Be open to renewing familiar patterns and friendships, but be ready to try new ways of living.

LIFE IS WORTH LIVING

Eventually we are able to think and talk about our loved one with happiness and a sense of peace. We have learned to accept the death, and can see options and possibilities for the future. We may experience renewed meaning in life. There is the possibility of emotional, spiritual, and personal growth. Often we become a different person—stronger, more involved, wiser, more compassionate, concerned, understanding, and aware. Our loved ones have entered a beautiful new life without pain and problems. We will be together someday. Meanwhile, they would want us to live this life to the fullest. Therefore, appreciate and enjoy this life and the people in this life. If we continue to love to the fullest, then his/her memory will be eternal.

APPENDIX C

ONE PARISH'S PASTORAL RESPONSE

THE CORPORAL WORKS OF MERCY

The Christian community is given a great responsibility, indeed, a mission to incorporate into its lifestyle the corporal works of mercy: feeding the hungry, giving drink to the thirsty, sheltering the homeless, clothing the naked, visiting the sick, visiting the imprisoned, and burying the dead. Each local community or parish is charged with the task of implementing these directives into their lived experience of faith-in-action. Naturally, each parish responds differently, depending upon its resources and the guidance of the Holy Spirit.

Like other parishes throughout the country, my parish—St. Margaret of Scotland community, a large suburban parish located on Long Island, New York—has tried to embrace these directives to the best of their ability. The reason is simple. Christians need to perform the works of mercy in order to become more like the Lord who is Mercy Incarnate. Unless we embrace these directives, we stifle the Spirit of God working within us. Therefore, we are called to embody the works of mercy so that the Lord's Body can be visible here in the world.

In reflecting upon the works of mercy, however, it is important to realize that the entire community is given this responsibility. It is not meant for certain individuals to "go it alone," but for the community itself, united by the Spirit in the Body of Christ, to perform the works of mercy. For that reason, we have tried to encourage individuals to embrace the works of mercy not as Lone Rangers, who happen to do good for others, but as representatives of God's people, who are striving to do good together. When visiting the sick, therefore, it means that we bring not just ourselves, but the entire community with us; when feeding the hungry we bring not just our own resources, but the combined resources of the entire community.

This understanding of the corporal works of mercy has challenged our parish to approach these directives with a different frame of mind, especially in the area of bereavement. Who, for example, is called to bury the dead? Is it simply the priest who attends the wake, celebrates the Mass of Christian Burial, and goes to the cemetery? This has been the practice for many years within most communities, although lay involvement with bereavement support groups has begun to increase.

At St. Margaret of Scotland parish, we needed, in some way, to acknowledge God's call to bury the dead, just as the parish had begun to accept God's call to feed the poor, visit the sick, etc. How to help others hear this call, however, remained the challenging question before us.

As often happens, we began slowly, taking tentative steps toward the goal. It started when the priests that were assigned to the parish found it impossible to be present at all the wakes scheduled at a particular time. In order to respond, therefore, we often contacted one or two parishioners, asking them to take care of a wake service at one funeral parlor while we tried to take care of two or three wake services at another. It was almost as if God were prepping us for an important "eureka" moment. Within a period of several months, we found ourselves calling parishioners repeatedly because the number of wake services scheduled for a particular day could not be accomplished by one priest. Admittedly, our initial reason for calling parishioners was to help the priest who could not accomplish the task that tradition-ally belonged to him. Within several months, however, we realized that our reasons for seeking help were incorrect. Parishioners needed not be called to help the priest accomplish his task; parishioners needed to be called so that they could fulfill their responsibility to perform the works of mercy.

Once the clergy became aware of and accepted this paradigm shift, the Lord seemed to pour his grace upon us. Within a short period of time, individuals came forward to help with the parish's Ministry of Hope program by being present to families during their griev-ing process. We already had an extensive aftercare program that involved counseling and bereavement sessions. These, however, required specialized training (which the parish willingly sponsored for those who had the necessary gifts).

Now, however, we saw that more people could get involved by simply being present in small ways during the actual wake period itself. We quickly organized groups of people who were able to visit the funeral parlor during the afternoon to help the family plan the funeral liturgy. We arranged for teams of two to four people to visit the funeral parlor during the evening, using that visit as an opportunity to lead those assembled in prayer, sharing, and reflection upon God's word. We called upon parishioners to join together on the day of burial so the family could be greeted at the church by members of the community, thus showing them in a physical way the presence of the Body of Christ—showing them that they were not alone in their hour of darkness.

Once the insight was accepted, the parish moved wholeheartedly in this direction, although we still encounter some families who insist that a priest be present. In such cases (which are relatively few), we try to respond with love and care, explaining that our parish family was very concerned with their expressed needs, and that we would do our best to fulfill those needs by having our Ministry of Hope wake team provide the prayers at the funeral parlor. In short, this has become a teachable moment for the parish and for those who are asked to give their loved one back to God. Although the initial reaction of some was that a priest needed to be present, the final experience was overwhelmingly positive as the grieving family experienced the care and compassion of the parish's Ministry of Hope wake team during the customary days of mourning.

In reflecting upon this development, the parish has become more aware of its interconnectedness, even at the time of death when families feel stripped of familiar

reference points. Having parishioners present for the
liturgy preparation, wake prayers, and funeral mass
enabled us to embrace those who mourn with the loving
presence of the Lord. This, in turn, has helped families
feel included in the community, even if they have been
away from the Eucharist for a substantial period of time.
Providing a faith-filled environment through the active
presence of the Ministry of Hope teams, we were able to
support those who felt that their faith was lacking or
weak or even missing.

WHAT IT LOOKS LIKE

At present, the parish has five teams of people who
are asked to serve for a particular period of time. We
continue to interpret the ongoing growth of this ministry
as a sign of God's grace working in our midst. No one, of
course, is asked to do something he/she cannot accomplish—for example, give a reflection—although all are
asked to stretch toward a non-preferred area of the
ministry so that God can use them as channels of grace
for others.

Each team comprises several people who have
certain responsibilities. One team member helps the
family arrange the liturgy by visiting the funeral parlor in
the afternoon, usually just before or after viewing hours.
The funeral director usually gives the family a small
parish-produced booklet containing the Scripture readings and song selections that might be used during the
Mass of Christian Burial. The team member then reviews
this material with the family, inviting members to

participate by reading the Scriptures, bringing gifts to the altar, etc.

Later that day, another two to four people assist with the prayers and reflection during the evening's wake service, making sure that the family is invited to participate through storytelling, eulogies, poetry, etc. Obviously, no family is forced to participate, but families are encouraged, knowing that for many, the telling of the story can have a healing effect upon those who are gathered.

Finally, another two or three parishioners attend the Mass of Christian Burial on the following day: greeting the guests, forming an "honor guard" to escort the family down the aisle, leading members of the congregation to the lectern should they choose to proclaim the readings, assisting participants during the offertory procession, guiding the communicants during the reception of the Eucharist, etc. In the near future, we hope to expand the teams further, so that the parish would be able to offer the Church's prayers of transferal as well as accompany the family to the place of burial.

Our Ministry of Hope program evolved from a simple aftercare program that was already in place for several years. By calling forth volunteers to write notes of condolences, especially during anniversary times, and by providing opportunities for individuals and families to work through their grief in a group process, our parish prepared itself to embrace more fully the call to bury the dead. It was as if the Spirit of God gradually prepared us to extend ourselves more and more to those in need. Nothing was done quickly or haphazardly. All was done with prayer and reflection. By taking these steps, one at a time, we have been able to extend the arms of Jesus to those in need. What has been most important, however, has been the realization that the arms of Jesus are not exclusively the arms of the ordained minister. They necessarily include the arms of the entire parish, with the ordained minister extending his arms primarily during the time of Eucharist, as we celebrate the dying and rising of the Lord whose Body we are.